While the author has made every effort to provide accurate, up-to-date source information at the time of publication, statistics and other data are constantly updated. Neither the publisher nor the author assumes any responsibility for errors or for changes that occur after publication. Further, the publisher and author do not have any control over and do not assume any responsibility for third-party websites or their content.

For more resources like this, visit charismahouse.com and the author's website at daystar.com.

Cataloging-in-Publication Data is on file with the Library of Congress. International Standard Book Number: 978-1-63641-375-4 E-book ISBN: 978-1-63641-376-1

1 2024
Printed in the United States of America

Most Charisma Media products are available at special quantity discounts for bulk purchase for sales promotions, premiums, fund-raising, and educational needs. For details, call us at (407) 333-0600 or visit our website at www.charismamedia.com.

The author has made every effort to provide accurate accounts of events, but she acknowledges that others may have different recollections of these events.

There are storms of this life still to be met, so get behind Christ by following him in the path of duty. *If you never go anywhere but where Christ leads the way, you need not be afraid of storms, for they will beat upon him more than upon you.*
—Charles Spurgeon

In order to realize the worth of the anchor we need to feel the stress of the storm.
—Corrie ten Boom

Then they cry out to the LORD *in their trouble, and He brings them out of their distresses. He calms the storm, so that its waves are still. Then they are glad because they are quiet; so He guides them to their desired haven. Oh, that men would give thanks to the* LORD *for His goodness, and for His wonderful works to the children of men!*
—David, Psalm 107:28–31

CONTENTS

Foreword

ONE OF MY favorite quotes is this: "Life doesn't form us. Our response to life forms us." I can't remember who I heard say that, but it's true. As a pastor for over forty years, I have personally witnessed the lives and spiritual journeys of thousands of believers. My greatest joy is to see people grow and succeed. My greatest pain is to see them fail and suffer. And in most cases, the difference maker is some form of difficulty or tragedy—a storm of life. From my perspective, believers are generally the same until they face an obstacle beyond their capacity to handle.

If life is a big classroom, then the storms of life are the tests to see what we've learned, or if we've learned. And who in the world likes storms? We all hate them and don't want them! But they are coming for all of us—the rich, the poor, the great, the average, the attractive, the normal, the mature, the immature, and so on. God never promised anyone a life without troubles and challenges. In fact, as you read your Bible, you will find that all the heroes of the faith had to endure storms—*big storms*! And the interesting thing is this: The greatest people in the Bible had to endure the greatest difficulties and challenges. And in every case, their testimony was preceded by a test—a storm. The same will be true for all of us.

One of the best modern-day examples of this point is Joni Lamb. I have known Joni for over twenty-five years. She is my precious sister in Christ, and she is a lioness of God. Joni is exactly the same person behind the scenes as she is on television, and that is one of the things I admire most about her. She is genuinely warm, kind, and compassionate, and she cares about everyone around her. You just feel better when you've been around Joni—whether you watch her on television or you're with her in person. She exudes the genuine love of Jesus.

But something about Joni that you might not notice as much on television is how strong she is. I'm not talking about a human type of strength. I'm talking about a strength that comes from tenaciously trusting God through the storms of life. I've walked with Joni through many storms over the past twenty-five years. Some of those storms you will read about in this book. And I can tell you firsthand that she is a woman of incredible faith!

You can know a person on a certain level in the good times. But you find out who a person really is in the bad times—the battles and storms! That is when a person's true character and faith (or lack of it) are exposed. And I know from walking with Joni through many challenges, difficulties, and crises that she is a true woman of God. Even in the darkest moments I have never seen her waver or compromise. But over and over I have watched her stand on God's Word and believe in His faithfulness with an overcomer's attitude and a determined faith.

I am so glad Joni decided to write this book, and I'm truly honored to be writing the foreword for my dear friend. You can be assured as you read this book that everything is true and nothing is hyped, airbrushed, or sensationalized. This is the real testimony of a modern-day champion of the faith. She has chosen to become vulnerable and allow all of us to see into the inner chambers of her life and the storms the Lord has brought her through. And the purpose of all this isn't to glorify a person but to glorify Jesus—and to let all of us know that He is with us in our storms and will be faithful to us if we trust in Him.

—JIMMY EVANS
FOUNDER AND PRESIDENT, XO MARRIAGE

Preface

SOMETHING'S COMING

JONI."

I snapped awake and sat straight up in bed.

"Joni." The voice called a second time, firm and distinct, spoken with authority, yet comforting, like a loving Father.

I glanced over at Marcus lying there. He was sound asleep. No one else was in the room or even close to the room, but there was no mistaking what I had heard. It was not my imagination, nor was I dreaming.

"Joni...Joni." The words were as tangible as if someone were standing by my bedside, calling for me. As I lay back staring at the ceiling, pondering what had just occurred, a holy awe settled over me. God had my ear. He had spoken my name.

"Yes, Lord. I'm here." I waited. There was no going back to sleep.

That morning, after I told Marcus what had happened, we both wondered what God was up to. Later, I asked our friend John Paul Jackson, whom God had used prophetically, "What does it mean when God calls your name out audibly?"

"Well," he said, "if the Lord speaks your name twice, He's trying to get your attention. He's wanting you to prepare for something that's coming."

The Lord had unmistakably spoken my name twice and definitely had my attention. The question was, Would I be prepared for what was coming?

Chapter 1

TAKE MY HAND

Lord, it's me, Joni, here—Your girl. Looks like I'm going through another storm, and this one is pretty rough. It's big—bigger than anything I've ever faced. You have to get me through this because if You don't, I'm going under, and the whole world is watching. I need You to show me what to do again. You've directed me my whole life and never failed me. You know I love You, Lord, and whatever You say, I'll do. But there are a lot of things and voices coming at me, so You have to make Your will crystal clear. I don't want to miss You."

"Take My hand, Joni. I'll show you as we go. Trust Me."

"OK, Lord."

You know, television is a funny thing. So much goes into the production process: you arrive at the studio early, you scurry to get makeup applied, bright lights shine in your face, directors point to where you need to stand and sit and look, crew run around like we're about to launch a rocket, camera people are on headsets, the clock counts down, guests are taken care of and lined up, and I pray—a lot—all kinds of prayers, out loud,

1

under my breath, with a group. "OK, Holy Spirit. We're ready. Let's do this." Lights, camera, action—*boom*. We're live on the air. The rocket has launched. And you know what? Right in the middle of all the commotion, the Holy Spirit shows up, and it's no longer a production. It's real. God moves.

He takes cracked vessels like this fiery girl from outside Greenville, South Carolina, and somehow uses her, along with all our other hosts, singers, guests, and crew. Lives are changed. People are drawn closer to Jesus and encouraged to keep going in the darkest of storms. We've received thousands of testimonies over the years, such as the one from a woman who was contemplating suicide. She had pills in her hand and was about to take them when the Lord led her to turn on the television. She found a Christian broadcast, and the guest spoke words that broke chains and strongholds. Instead of committing suicide, she was set free. That's the core of why we do what we do.

On the air I've always tried to be real, letting you see the authentic me, even when I was going through my own turbulent storms—and there have been many. Still, viewers only get to see a part of me. That's just the nature of television. There are so many things going on behind the scenes, where the cameras aren't rolling. In this book, however, we're going to walk back through some of my most challenging storms so you can get the whole story—the real story. I'm not holding back. We're talking about personal betrayal, false accusations, public humiliation, ridiculous lawsuits (by the way, we've never lost a single one in forty years), Marcus' and my journey, his death, a car accident caused by a drunk driver that should have left me dead, and more. Yet you're also going to see God's sustaining peace, resurrection power, and loving restoration at work, along with some startling answers to prayer when I needed the Lord to come through the most. We believed God, we stood on His Word, and we overcame.

I've often said, as many others have, in life you are either in a storm, coming out of a storm, or about to enter a storm. The difference between most of you and me, though, is when I go through a storm, the whole world sees—and everyone has an opinion. It makes me feel raw and exposed. More often than not, people's opinions are based on partial or distorted information. Plus, they haven't seen all my late-night conversations with God and how I cried out to Him in the wee hours of the morning. They haven't seen those private times in the midst of deep grief and heartache, uncertainty and confusion, when I cried until I couldn't cry anymore.

Sometimes tears are the only way to express the anguish; words just won't do. Then, when the tears dry up, we resort to eating too much ice cream and pulling the pillow over our heads, trying to find a bit of sleep. It is not a pretty sight. Suddenly, right there in that blurry moment of desperation, the Lord speaks. On rare occasions His voice is loud and thundering; it may even be audible. But most of the time it's a quiet and gentle whisper from somewhere down in your innermost being, saying, "Trust Me."

With it comes a peace that passes all understanding and, finally, sleep. The next morning we have courage that's greater than us to get up and go do ministry again, to put ourselves out there before the world, knowing we're vulnerable. We go complete the assignment God gave us, even when we're exhausted and all we want to do is hide somewhere. All the while, we have peace and a knowing that the Lord has us. My good friend Rhonda, who was also in public ministry when she lost her husband, spoke almost those exact words to me many times. She and I had many late-night conversations and determined we would keep getting up, showing up, and trusting God in the process.

Ever since Marcus and I started building our first station back in 1984 with nothing but a mustard seed of faith and a vision from God, our purpose was to spread the gospel, encourage believers in their walk, and help the hurting. That has always been our vision, whether we were on television, leading crusades, engaging in missions—or even in a hospital room.

Once, while building our second station in Dallas, two workers fell three hundred feet from the KMPX tower that was under construction. We were called and told there had been a terrible accident with possible deaths. But God intervened, and both men survived. At the hospital we even led one of the men and his girlfriend to the Lord! The worker had a dream of an angel catching him in his lap as he fell. This was a true miracle that happened right before our eyes.

This story encapsulates my life and ministry. We are using television to reach the masses, but that day God used us in the hospital room to touch a few hurting individuals. God is all about reaching the one. What's interesting about TV ministry is it reaches the masses while at the same time touching viewers individually in their homes and hearts.

For nearly forty years the Lord has carried me through countless storms when by all outward appearances it looked as if I were going under. Fear would try to overtake me, along with doubt and apprehension, but I always knew God was there and I could trust Him. Some days we're just tired and worn-out, but the Lord is faithful to give us strength when we are weak.

I've also witnessed how the Lord has delivered and empowered so many of the incredible men and women of God I've been honored to get to know over thirty-eight years of TV ministry. Many of those I've interviewed have become friends and great sources of inspiration for me, people such as John Paul Jackson, Jimmy Evans, and Jonathan Cahn—there are too many to name. You will meet some of them in the following pages. I can't put a price tag on their encouragement and wisdom.

All of us can be empowered by hearing others' God stories. Revelation 12:11 tells us they overcame "by the blood of the Lamb and by the word of their testimony." Something powerful happens when we hear stories of other people who have overcome. Testimonies are irresistible. That's the underlying motivation for *Joni Table Talk*.

The Lord has never failed me. He has led me through His Word, His Spirit, godly counsel, and wise friends. He's been my anchor and lighthouse through some of the most heart-wrenching, violent storms, and He has always seen me through to the new beginnings on the other side. We are going to talk about some of those new beginnings later.

In these past forty years, I have gained a calm assurance that we can absolutely trust God in the most turbulent of circumstances. Not only that, but with each storm He brings us through, we grow stronger in that trust. It's like a notch in our life belts. It's not that we are somehow better than others; we are still human vessels, but our trust becomes more secure in Him.

We can't survive life's storms or accomplish His will in our own power and ability. In fact, most of the time His plans are so big we can't achieve them without Him. If our goal is not bigger than we are, it's probably not God. His Word says, "'My grace is sufficient for you, for my power is made perfect in weakness.' Therefore I will boast all the more gladly about my weaknesses, so that Christ's power may rest on me" (2 Cor. 12:9, NIV).

Thankfully, none of us have to go through our storms alone. Jesus shows up on the raging waters holding out His hand, saying, "Take it. Trust Me. I've got you." But we have to grab hold and not let go. My grandfather Trammell told me many times when I was growing up, "Joni, hold tight to His hand. You will have to be the one to let go because He never will." Jesus said, "In the world you have tribulation and distress and suffering." That's a promise I guarantee not many of us have taped on the bathroom mirror. Yet Jesus continued by saying, "But be courageous [be confident, be undaunted, be filled with joy]; I have overcome the world" (John 16:33, AMP).

Jesus began John 16:33 with the greatest promise of all: "I have told you these things, so that in Me you may have [perfect] peace" (AMP). I certainly don't have all the answers to the zillion *why* questions, but Jesus promises not just peace but "perfect peace" in the midst of extreme distress and suffering. He is real and fully present, even when we don't feel Him. He sees and listens. He hears our cries, and He directs. My wounds sting like everyone else's. Yet the Lord is teaching me day by day to take courage in His power, grab hold of His hand as Grandpa told me, and trust Him when everything around me screams I'm going under.

I've felt that perfect peace when by all human reasonableness I should have been in deep depression and despair. But I wasn't. I've learned firsthand that joy really does come in the morning. This is my life story, and I assure you it's the real story. In addition, peppered throughout this book are teaching nuggets I've gleaned over the years. My prayer is that this book gives you a glimpse into another side of me, but more importantly that it moves you a little closer to Jesus and encourages you to grab His outstretched hand when you're in the midst of your own storms. He's waiting for you to take it.

STEPS THROUGH THE STORM

When you pass through waters, I will be with you.
And through the rivers, they shall not overflow you.
—ISAIAH 43:2, MEV

Once, when Jesus and the disciples were out at sea, a violent storm hit. By all outward appearances it looked as if they were going under. Yet Jesus was inside the boat, fast asleep. "Teacher," they cried, "do You not care that we are perishing?" (Mark 4:38). Isn't that just like us? When our lives are being pounded by turbulence, we're convinced Jesus is sleeping and doesn't care about our struggles. Nothing could be further from the truth. Jesus was never unaware of the disciples' situation. He could sleep peacefully while the storm raged because He knew what their end would be. He knew the storm would cease at just His word and they would reach the other side safely.

THROUGH THE STORM

Jesus knows about your storms too and is fully present with you. You are safe in His arms. When you pass through waters, He will be with you. By choosing to believe His promise and trust Him, you can exhale and enjoy the voyage.

Lord, my prayer today is simple: Help me see You in my storm and trust You as I cling to Your promises. Calm my anxiety and fill me with rest, helping me know You are aware of the situation and in total control. I trust that You will faithfully bring me to the other side. Amen.

Chapter 2

HIS PERFECT WILL
IN THE STORM

DEAR LORD, TAKE my life. Use me in whatever way, and I pray You show me the path to follow. I know I don't always understand, but Lord, I know You loved me enough to die for me. Oh, God, I put my faith in You, and I know with Your hand my life can be in Your perfect will. I pray I can be close to You always. I love You, Lord Jesus. Thank You for hearing my prayer."

I wrote those words in a letter on July 21, 1980, at 11:26 p.m., when I was twenty years old. Though I tucked it under my mattress, that letter represented a defining moment for me. But I'll get to that.

Back in 1980, I loved two men, neither of whom was Marcus Lamb. I had not met him yet, but the Lord would totally set me up.

The first of those two men was Jesus. Now, I can just imagine some of you rolling your eyes as you read that. But I'm not at all wanting to romanticize the past or sound super spiritual.

That is simply a true statement that is critical to my life story. I received Jesus as a child and was baptized in the Holy Spirit at thirteen. From then on, I loved my church and being with God's people. I was involved in the youth group and the youth choir, sang in the church choir, and even taught a Sunday school class to second-grade kids. I didn't do it because I had to; I did it because I got to! Serving was an important part of my spiritual growth.

Most importantly, though, Jesus had captured my heart and drawn me into an intimate relationship with Him that would sustain me my whole life. Pastor Robert Morris of Gateway Church once said having a testimony that you came to Jesus early in life is just as powerful as having a testimony of being delivered from a life of deep rebellion. He has a great sense of humor. He said he was delivered from drugs while his wife was delivered from M&M's, but her testimony is just as powerful. I guess I was more like Robert Morris' wife, Debbie. Having said that, I was still a strong-willed teenager who had questions and dealt with fitting in like most young girls. The truth is, I just loved Jesus, and the Holy Spirit gave me a sense of right and wrong that would prevent me from making some seriously poor choices. He protected me.

One of the things that impacted me early on was that my dad and I participated in the bus ministry together. I was around twelve years old at the time. We picked up kids in poor neighborhoods, and the experience really opened my eyes to the hurts and struggles that some go through. We'd get up early on Saturday mornings and drive to some of the neighborhoods where families had very little. They would invite us in, and we'd sit down on their worn and broken-down furniture.

We could see their clothes were ragged and worn too. I'd find myself fighting back the tears because their situation would break my heart.

My dad and I would meet the parents, or the parent, and say, "Hey, we'd love to be able to take your children to church." Then we'd come back on Sunday morning and pick them up. On the way, I would do a little Bible lesson on the bus. That was a life-changing time. Jesus was not, and is not, a churchy, religious figure to me. He is real, and I began encountering Him in my youth.

I'm grateful for my godly parents, who laid a solid foundation for me and my three siblings. I grew up seeing love and physical affection. It wasn't uncommon to watch my dad sneak up behind my mom while she was cooking and squeeze her. Those sweet moments gave me a warm feeling and a sense of security. I never had trouble believing my heavenly Father loved me. My earthly father gave me my first glimpse of my heavenly Father, and I'm thankful for that.

In high school I never wanted to be perceived as preachy or a goody-goody, holier-than-thou type. I hated that stereotype and tried to be real. What you saw was what you got, and the Jesus inside me couldn't help seeping out. A perfect example is one day during my senior year a bunch of us were hanging out around the library and somehow the subject turned to the Bible.

One of my dear friends, Dan—who, by the way, was one of the smartest guys in the school—spoke up and said, "You know the stories in the Bible are just poetic and didn't really happen. They're just fairy tales." Something rose up from inside me, and I shot back in front of all my friends, "Oh, they're real, all right. The Bible is God's Word. It's not a fairy tale. Noah and the ark actually happened. And Jonah and the whale really happened."

There were a few chuckles from the others, but I was passionate and didn't really care what anybody thought. It was just who I was. Listen to what happened, though. One day years later, after I was married to Marcus and we were living in Alabama, fully immersed in ministry, the phone rang, and I picked it up. (We had landlines back then.)

"Hello?" I said.

"Is Joni there?" the voice asked.

"This is Joni."

"Joni, this is Dan."

"Hey, Dan. What in the world?" I said. "How did you find me?"

He said, "I had to find you." And then he told me he had gotten saved. "You're one of two people I wanted to track down and find," he added. "I'll never forget what happened in the library that day, your passion for believing the Bible is true."

That story is an example of how God seems to work in my life. I'm not a scholar, though I do study the Word. I'm not a preacher, though sometimes He uses me that way. I'm just Joni. I try to be available, and the Lord is fine with that. Jesus has never failed me—never—and He won't fail you either.

Of course, coming out of high school, I was your typical young woman with her whole life ahead of her. Tall, skinny, and as I already mentioned, strong-willed, I had a four-cylinder Ford Mustang that I drove like an eight-cylinder. I'd be in the car with the pedal to the metal while singing away at the top of my lungs. When I played softball, I did it in the same pedal-to-the-metal way. I was that scrappy left fielder or short-stop always diving for the ball. You could say I was maybe a little competitive. In my youthful fervency, I would bump into things and people from time to time too. You get the picture. If I was going to serve Jesus, I wanted to go all out too. However, that love and passion would be tested.

Keep in mind, in 1980, when I penned the letter I shared at the beginning of this chapter, I had no vision for a television ministry, or any kind of full-time ministry, for that matter. There was no Marcus Lamb in the plan. I was working at an engineering firm and dreamed of marriage and a family. Still, down in my heart of hearts, I wanted God's will and His best for my life. The letter I wrote to the Lord was maybe a bit youthfully dramatic, but it was intimate, just between God and me. It wasn't for show, and the only reason I put it in this book all these years later is to demonstrate where I was in my relationship with Him. The letter showed me surrendering my will to His at a critical juncture in my life. I didn't even realize how powerful that prayer was, but the Lord took it seriously. He took me at my word. He will also take you at your word.

I wrote about this extensively in my first book, *Surrender All*. That book was written fifteen years ago, and it's important that I revisit the story for this book. But I want to address it from a slightly different angle: Obedience to the Lord often puts us smack-dab in the middle of a storm. However, if you experience a storm as a result of obedience, just know God has something better on the other side—so much better.

You see, writing that letter and laying down my will had to do with the *second* man I was in love with at that time. He was charming, rugged, and fun, and we'd been dating seriously from the time I was eighteen. It had been over a year, and I hoped we were moving in the direction of marriage. My dream was to get married, have a home, and raise a family. I wanted a man to come up from behind me and hug me as my dad did my mom. That's what I wanted, and there's nothing wrong with that. *Unless...*

DISCOVERING THE VOICE OF THE LORD

At that time in my life, I felt a strange uneasiness gnawing at my spirit. Over the years, I've come to know that as the voice of the Holy Spirit. It's an inner prompting, a nudge, an uneasiness, or a confirming peace that has become more honed as I've grown in my relationship with God. Sometimes it's a gentle whisper that cuts through all the noise and other voices, even my own.

Concerning the man I thought I loved, God was letting me know this person was not His perfect will for me. But oh, how I wanted him to be! My pastor's wife confirmed the word the Holy Spirit had dropped in my spirit when she came to me and said, "I know God has a plan for your life, Joni." And then she tenderly told me, "I don't think this person is God's will for you. We love you and are praying for you." I remember thinking at the time, "I'm not listening. I don't want to hear that." But a seed was planted that I would recall later when I wrote my letter to the Lord.

When I tucked the letter under my bed that night, I was hoping the Lord would say, "This was a test, Joni. You go ahead with your plan." Yet that's not what happened. The uneasiness inside me grew even stronger, and I knew what that meant. The

Holy Spirit was directing me to make a choice. I had written in the letter that I wanted God's perfect will. Did I really mean it?

The Lord's answer was simply, "Obey Me." Those words kept ringing in my spirit: "Obey Me." I knew what I had to do: break it off and trust that God had something better. I had no idea what was in my future. It's easy to make a decision when we know what's waiting on the other side of obedience, but when we don't know what's on the other side and we choose to obey just because we love God, that's when the Lord knows He can really trust us. Will we be obedient when we don't know what the future holds? That's real trust.

Needless to say, my guy didn't take it very well. There were shouts and hurtful things said. There was pain, and there were tears. He yelled, "You take your God and—" Well, you get the idea. That was an eye-opener and confirmation that he was not the one for me. Nevertheless I still felt guilty, as if a piece of me had broken off for letting him go. One thing was sure, though: the ordeal made it crystal clear that I was making the right choice.

As time passed, he moved on and married a nice girl and started a family. The breakup wasn't catastrophic compared with the devastating storms some have experienced or that I would eventually experience, but in that season in my life I still considered it a traumatic storm. I was beginning to learn what it meant to trust the Lord and be obedient through the turbulence.

Some storms are big, and some are small. They can be category 5 hurricanes or local thunderstorms. Either way, God wants us to trust Him. Small storms can feel big, though. They're like having a flat tire on a busy interstate. It's not a big deal when compared with things like the death of a child or spouse, or when the doctor utters the words, "It's cancer." Yet a flat tire is terribly inconvenient and frustrating, especially when it's raining. It's messy, and your whole life stops until the issue is resolved and you get going again.

Those unexpected delays seem to have a special way of testing our patience and trust. These delays don't necessarily mean denial, as though you are out of God's will. They actually can be God's protection. I knew a man who got a flat tire and was so upset because of the delay it caused. When he finally got back on the road, he came upon a serious accident involving several vehicles, and it quite possibly could have involved him and his family had they not been delayed.

Some storms are like that. God actually uses them to guide and even protect us. It's when we try to do life on our own that we mess up, and sometimes our mess-ups create storms. The good news is even when we botch things, as I definitely have on a number of occasions, God's grace is bigger. He specializes in turning our messes into masterpieces and messages.

On occasion, however, God calls us right into the storm. The storm in Noah's life started way before the rain did. It started when he said yes to God and began building the ark. Things got pretty tough for Noah, but his obedience saved his family and all of humanity. God was right there guiding when Joseph was in the storm of being thrown in the pit, sold into slavery, falsely accused, and imprisoned for fourteen years. This was the path that would lead Joseph to walking in God's dream for his life and saving his family, the children of Israel, in the process. Once he was on the other side, Joseph was able to look at his brothers who had betrayed him and say, "But as for you, you meant evil against me; but God meant it for good, in order to bring it about as it is this day, to save many people alive" (Gen. 50:20).

Joseph was in God's perfect will all the time he was in the storm of slavery and prison in Egypt, and he remained faithful. It's while we're in the midst of the turbulence that trust and faith are critical, because if you really believe God is holding you in the palm of His hand, you can rest in the reality that He sees you and is in the process of bringing you through to the other side. The problem is, dark skies, thunder and lightning, cutting wind and rain, and raging waves keep us from seeing the other side. The storm can be quite scary, especially when we can't see the Lord. Yet that's when He whispers through the gale, "Trust Me. I see something that you don't see. It's coming. Hold My hand."

When Jesus told His disciples to meet Him on the other side of the sea, He knew perfectly well that they were going right into the middle of a life-threatening, boat-sinking kind of storm. After all, He was God wrapped in flesh. The disciples were simply obeying Jesus' command, yet they ended up in a storm so bad they feared for their lives. Amid the wind and waves they saw Jesus walking toward them on the water. The disciples saw miracles they never would have known outside the storm, such as Jesus calming the waves and Peter walking on the water. So don't think for a minute that being in the storm means you've been disobedient or that you lack faith. That is not the case. Jesus just wants you to take His outstretched hand.

Breaking up with that young man created turbulence in my young life. Yet if I hadn't obeyed the Lord's prompting, I would have married the wrong guy. Yes, God could have shown up in that marriage; He specializes in redeeming our mistakes. But I would have missed His best for me, which was marrying Marcus, leading the ministry God had for me, and raising my children.

Eventually Daystar would reach millions of viewers and lead me to my current position as ministry president. Saying yes to the Lord sometimes creates turbulence, but on the other side of the storm is something better—so much better. If you know you are making a wrong decision, put on your brakes, turn around, and make the choice you know will please the heart of God. You won't regret it.

STEPS THROUGH THE STORM

If we live in the Spirit, let us also walk in the Spirit.
—GALATIANS 5:25

If a storm comes as a result of your obedience, you can be sure of one thing: the Lord isn't sending you into the situation alone. He is with you and will go before you, making a way. He is the waymaker. He's opening doors you couldn't even imagine before you chose to step out in faith. This storm is pushing you right into His perfect will, and that's a place where you want to be, even if it's hard sometimes. All storms pass, and when this one does, you will be so glad you chose obedience.

When you sense the Holy Spirit nudging you to make a move and do something uncomfortable or out of the norm, do you trust Him enough to act on it? His nudges will always line up with the Word of God, and if you follow them, you'll be glad you did. God's plans for your life are good (Jer. 29:11).

> *Lord, my desire is to please You in everything I do. Help me listen and hear Your still, small voice. Show me what You want me to do, and grant me the strength to obey. Amen.*

Chapter 3

SNOWFLAKES AND WEDDING CAKE

S NOWFLAKES. I BET you didn't see that one coming. We'll get to the wedding cake later. But what in the world do snowflakes have to do with courageous faith in turbulent times, and particularly with my life story? More than you may realize.

If you look at a random snowflake under a magnifying glass or microscope, you'll immediately see they are not random at all. Rather, they are exquisite, complex, perfectly formed, ice crystal–kaleidoscope works of art. Snowflakes scream there's a Creator. David Jeremiah, a best-selling author and spiritual father to millions, said: "Those tiny, temporary wisps of ice we call snowflakes are a wonder of creation. They are the artwork of the heavens, God's celestial geometry."[1]

It is commonly said that while they are similar, no two snowflakes are identical. But there's something else that I'd bet you didn't know about snowflakes. An individual snow-flake begins as a tiny droplet of supercooled water that freezes in the sky to create an ice crystal. However, snowflakes are shaped into their mesmerizing designs as they fall from the sky some ten thousand feet above the earth. While they are falling, these tiny pieces of frozen water are buffeted by the atmospheric conditions. The wind, pressure, and temperature create turbulence that actually works together with the hand of God to chisel these unique and beautiful patterns.[2] You can see where I'm going with this. In other words, a snowflake's beauty and design are shaped by turbulence and storms. And because every snowflake has a completely unique journey to earth, each one is shaped a bit differently.

Poet and writer Angie Weiland-Crosby wrote, "I am built of snowflakes with your touch; a million storied diamonds in the rough."[3] Just like snowflakes, all humans are similar while at the same time being unique, having individual DNA, fingerprints, and personalities. The Lord told Jeremiah, "Before I formed you in the womb I knew you, before you were born *I set you apart*; I appointed you as a prophet to the nations" (Jer. 1:5, NIV, emphasis added).

The Lord was talking to Jeremiah about his specific calling as a prophet; however, the same holds true for us. God knew us, formed us uniquely, and set us apart for a distinct purpose. I can prove it. Consider these fascinating words from the apostle Paul:

> And He [God] has made from one blood every nation of men to dwell on all the face of the earth, and has determined their preappointed times and the boundaries of their dwellings, so that they should seek the Lord, in the hope that they might grope for Him and find Him, though He is not far from each one of us; for in Him we live and move and have our being.
>
> —ACTS 17:26–28

Wow. Can you believe that? Not only did God specifically make you, but He also specifically placed you in this exact moment and location in time. This is how I met Marcus. God had me at the right place at the right time.

God knows where you are because in Him you live and move and have your being. That means your challenging storms are in Him too. God is that big. The whole universe is inside Him. Yet He is as close as your breath so you would grope for Him and find Him, especially in your storms. The biblical meaning of *grope* is to reach and feel around for something desperately, like one in darkness.[4] God wants us to reach out and find Him in our darkest moments. He is there. Jesus led the disciples into that storm on the Sea of Galilee so they would find out that He was right there with them and they could trust Him, that He was never out of control. After breaking it off with the man I thought was "the one," I drove away crying and just wanted to bury myself under a pillow and blankets. I would soon find out the Lord was never more in control than He was then.

Bruce Van Natta has been a guest on Daystar a couple of times. His is one of the most amazing and most documented miracles in the world. Bruce's story demonstrates my point perfectly. He was a diesel mechanic in a small country town in Wisconsin, living a normal, routine life. He got up in the mornings, ate breakfast, went to work, took a lunch break, went back to work fixing engines, washed up with degreasing soap, and then went home to his wife and kids. He wasn't a major evangelist or TV minister. He didn't pastor a large church or write books. He was a regular Joe. Yet, as with every one of us, God was right there with him in a most violent storm.

One day Bruce was working underneath a diesel truck, as he'd done nearly every day for years, when the jack gave way and the 18-wheeler collapsed on him. The axle of the several-ton truck crushed his body, severing five major arteries and pulverizing his stomach and intestines. Bruce died on the scene. You could say that was a major storm. Yet Bruce's spirit was never more alive. In fact, he was in absolute peace as he watched the whole scene unfold below him. He saw the paramedics and later recalled distinct, verified details he should not have known because he was unconscious. What's even more startling is Bruce also saw two massive, ten-foot glowing angels on both sides of his flattened body. With tears in his eyes, Bruce said in an interview that the angels were not hazy images. They were as clear as a person standing right next to him. It was the most real experience of his life.

Then, as Bruce's spirit started ascending, he heard God's voice asking him if he wanted to go back but also telling him if he did, it wasn't going to be easy. Bruce felt so much peace that he didn't want to go back, but then he thought of his wife and children and said he would return. At that moment, he woke up in his body, shocking the paramedic.[5] You can read his story in his book *A Miraculous Life.* My point in telling you this is that even in the midst of that tragic accident that by all natural appearances shouted God was absent, the exact opposite was true. God was never nearer. He was as fully present to Bruce, a back-roads diesel mechanic, as He was to Billy Graham or Charles Spurgeon. Remember, the presence of pain does not mean the absence of God.

I don't understand how He does it, but God is able to be fully present with me and billions of others throughout time simultaneously without being diminished. He is outside time and the reality of this dimension. God sees time past, time present, and time future simultaneously. Theologian A. W. Tozer wrote, "God dwells in His creation and is everywhere indivisibly present. Wherever we are, God is here. No point is nearer to God than any other point."[6] The psalmist put it this way: "Where can I go from your Spirit? Where can I flee from your presence?...For you created my inmost being; you knit me together in my mother's womb" (Ps. 139:7, 13, NIV). Do you see that? God's omnipotent presence is directly linked to your personal creation. God knows you and knows exactly what you are going through.

Also, as with a snowflake, the turbulence along our journey is uniquely shaping and making us. God certainly doesn't cause painful and difficult things. We live in a fallen, sinful world that is groaning for the day of redemption. Jesus, God in the flesh, came to this planet and suffered and died as one of us to redeem us and deal with the enemy of our souls and the sin of mankind. There is a reason God is allowing evil and pain to run its course. One day He will put a complete end to it. In the meantime, though, God is using everything, even the turbulence and storms in our lives, to form us. "And we know that all things work together for good to those who love God, to those who are the called according to His purpose" (Rom. 8:28).

The last time I checked, *all* means *all*, including storms. But what is the snowflake-like design we are being formed into? We are being shaped and molded into the image of Christ while retaining our individual personalities. Your whole life is ultimately about you uniquely becoming more like Jesus. (See Galatians 4:19–20.)

Don't get me wrong—there are many happy moments we celebrate and enjoy in this life. God uses them too. He wants us to be content and fulfilled, walking in our destiny. He wants to give us a future and a hope. Life is not all about storms. This is not a negative, downer message. Yet the reality is we live in a fallen, messed-up world where painful, frustrating, and overwhelming stuff happens. Christianity is not a self-help course. Jesus isn't about us being happy, happy, happy all the time. He's about giving us peace, joy, and strength in whatever circumstance in which we find ourselves. Happiness is determined by our circumstances; peace and joy are not. Though it may be dark right now, joy will come in the morning.

Along with being created uniquely, each one of us is at a unique season in our lives, and the storms and promptings of the Holy Spirit are particular to that season. Some seasons are more turbulent than others, but all are equally important. The way we respond has everything to do with how we move forward, even if our response is simply holding on to the Father's hand, crawling into His lap, and trusting Him. Sometimes that's all we can do. The Lord knows that.

WHO'S THAT GIRL?

When I said yes to the Lord back in 1980, little did I realize it would set a domino effect into motion that would alter the course of my life. Breaking off my relationship was devastating on a certain level in that season of life. Revival had been going on all week at our church, the Tremont Avenue Church of God; however, I was busy at work and trying to move on. My mom called me at work on Wednesday afternoon (I had worked late Monday and Tuesday) and said, "Honey, you should come to the revival tonight. It's been really great." So I went that night. It just so happened that the revival was being conducted by a dynamic young evangelist out of Lee University named Marcus Lamb.

What you have to understand, though, is when I went to church that night, I wasn't thinking I'd meet someone. I wasn't thinking, "Wow, look at that guy." I was still grieving. Plus, our church had a regular attendance of about a thousand, and it was pretty full. I was just another girl in the congregation. I had no thoughts of dating anyone at that time.

Unbeknownst to me, Marcus had spotted me in the crowd and leaned over to our music director, Mike, and asked, "Who's that girl?"

"That's Joni Trammell," Mike said.

After the service there were hot dogs and snacks in the dining hall, and several girls flocked around Marcus, crushing on him. He was handsome and seemed to have a fun personality. I was back in the kitchen, keeping my distance, not really interested. Really, I just wanted to go home and spend time with my pillow. Marcus, however, wanted to meet me, and my girlfriend insisted that I go talk to him. I resisted until she finally dragged me out there. Marcus introduced himself, we had a friendly exchange, and I went home. The next night, I was standing near the platform while he was playing the piano at the end of the service, and he leaned over and asked me, "Hey, would you like to go get pizza with Mike and Cindy?" I was surprised but intrigued. I thought, "I've never dated a preacher, but OK."

To my surprise, Marcus was kind, funny, and refreshing. I had never gone out with someone so committed and surrendered to God. We held the same values, and I was at ease in his presence. Marcus asked me out every night of the revival. That weekend, I met his parents and his brother, Gary, who lived in Georgia. I loved his family, and he fell in love with my family as well. Over time we fell in love. On Valentine's Day 1982 he proposed, and I said yes. Nearly six months later, on August 6, 1982, we were married at my home church in Greenville, South Carolina.

It was a whirlwind first year as I was thrust into the life of an evangelist's wife. I ended up traveling with Marcus for about two years. At first I was primarily in a support role to my husband, but that role would soon grow and become more public. After that I began praying with people at the altar and singing before he preached. In March 1983, seven months after our wedding, we were in the Holy Land, a trip gifted to us by a pastor close to Marcus. While we were there, the Lord spoke to Marcus on the Mount of Olives and instructed us to get involved in Christian television.

Soon we were given an opportunity to move to Montgomery, Alabama, to help build the first full-power Christian TV station in the state. That move would change the trajectory of our lives, so for the next five months we prayed about it.

In August 1983, on our one-year anniversary, instead of eating the top of our wedding cake as we had planned, we went on a three-day fast to make sure God wanted us to move forward with helping build the Christian station in Montgomery. The funny part of that story is that I had never done a three-day fast with no food, and I thought, "Oh my goodness, I'm dying. I'm not going to make it." I'd never gone through anything like that, but Marcus had done many fasts, and he laughed at me because it was kind of funny. At the end of the fast, we both had an assurance that we were supposed to go to Alabama. God had said yes.

The Montgomery station first came on our radar after Marcus held a revival in that city. The pastor of the church there had a permit to build Channel 45, but he was having difficulty getting it off the ground. Marcus found out about the permit to build the station and connected the pastor with another group that had already built a Christian station. These people secured the permit from the pastor and began to talk to us about moving to Montgomery to help them build the station. They also wanted us to host their nightly show.

It turned out they didn't have the money to build the station, and the local congregation was disappointed that the TV station had not materialized. But in the end the Lord opened the door for Marcus and me to build the station. This time obedience would require laying everything down and stepping out in faith. Marcus started putting our own money into the project, money he had saved while ministering as an evangelist. Eventually we built the station, although rather poorly, from old equipment and a transmitter from the garbage dump. When I think about it now, it's laughable that we even got on the air. My dad, Marcus' dad, and some friends borrowed money to help us get Channel 45 on the air. It was truly a miracle.

There would be storms of ridicule, poor advice, lies, and lack of finances. I mean, who starts a Christian TV station with no money in a place like Montgomery? How do you raise a family? Honestly, we knew it better have been God speaking to us because otherwise what we were doing would have been crazy. One time a well-known international preacher with a television ministry visited our fledgling station after we asked him to come and pray over it. Later he told mutual friends, "That couple doesn't know what they are doing, and that TV station will never get on the air!" Did we really hear from God? The theme of our lives seemed to be, "Marcus, Joni, take My hand. Trust Me as we walk through this." We did, and He has been faithful every time.

Most people have a concept of Daystar based on what they see today. They didn't see the many years of leanness and struggle that God brought us through to get here—all the times we had to walk through difficult situations and trust God for daily manna not only for the station but also for our family. If God didn't come through daily, we were in trouble. Once Daystar had grown and Marcus and I were walking in our destiny, we were able to help others. Considering the life of Joseph again, only when God finally brought him out of bondage and into his ultimate destiny was Joseph able to help his family, preserve God's plan to grow the people of Israel, and even save Pharaoh and Egypt.

While I was writing this chapter, the nation of Israel came under one of the most brutal attacks in its history. It was an unprecedented storm for them, perhaps the worst since the Holocaust. We at Daystar were able to respond by sending millions of dollars in aid, supplies, and spiritual support. We rearranged our regular programming to facilitate a response to Israel's crisis. We've reached out to others in their times of crisis too. We've given millions of dollars to churches and ministries such as the Dream Center in Los Angeles. When Hurricane Katrina hit, Daystar gave $2.5 million in relief for the victims. When people are going through storms, we should always pray for them, and at times we are called to come alongside them. To do so, we may have to rearrange some things. When God brings us through storms and we get stronger, we are able to help others in their times of need.

You can be in the midst of a storm and still be moving in your destiny. The presence of storms and pain doesn't mean you are out of God's will. It doesn't mean He is absent. In fact, you might be right in the middle of the will of God during your most violent storm. This is not necessarily the most popular thing to say, but it is the truth, and I'm going to be real with you. God uses storms to refine us and get us where He ultimately wants us to be.

It can be a struggle to believe that God is moving and guiding us through storms. But we must remember that when the Lord prompts us to do things, He is working outside of time. He knows the end and the beginning. He has a divine plan, but it is revealed to us step by step as we move forward in our journey. Our lives are like that falling snowflake being perfectly formed. A twenty-year-old being prompted to break up with her boyfriend seems trivial to some, but that decision was just as important as the one I made while on my knees, crying out to God for direction after Marcus was laid in the ground. We'll get to that.

Steps Through the Storm

My brethren, count it all joy when you fall into various trials, knowing that the testing of your faith produces patience. But let patience have its perfect work, that you may be perfect and complete, lacking nothing.

—James 1:2–4

31

THROUGH THE STORM

When we trust the Lord in our storms, we are letting Him use those trials to mold us into His image. He is not causing the storms; again, they are a result of living in this fallen, broken world. Still, the Lord uses the pressure as a tool in His hands to refine our character. The people in your life are not always the ones you want, but they are the ones you need to help make you the person you were meant to be.

Sometimes we have to go through the storm to appreciate the sunshine. In addition, going through turbulent waters refocuses us on the things that matter most. Storms have a way of uniting families and communities. During those times, our attention turns away from ourselves to the well-being of those we love. Things that don't really matter get tossed overboard. James said the testing of our faith produces patience. God takes us through that process so we "may be perfect and complete, lacking nothing."

> *Lord, use this storm to refine me and refocus me on what's important. I thank You for the people You have placed around me and for using them to develop Your character in me. Let me love and serve those You have put in my path. Amen.*

Chapter 4

PEACE, BE STILL

I THINK I MUST have come out of my mother's womb with my hands raised high, singing hallelujah. My first-grade teacher wrote on my report card, "Joni's so amusing in the music class because she sings louder than everyone else." Music and singing have always been foundational to who I am, particularly worship. From a very young age I've loved communing with the Lord through song. I did that long before there was any television or public ministry.

When I was thirteen, I had an open vision in my room while worshipping the Lord with a hairbrush in my hand, pretending it was a microphone. (I believe all true singers have used their hairbrushes as microphones at some point!) Suddenly I saw myself leading worship in front of thousands and thousands of people. Though the scene was unfolding in my mind's eye, it was as if I were right there. What's interesting is that I hadn't been thinking about leading worship in front of thousands of people or anything like that. I didn't even have a tangible concept of singers and musicians leading worship before massive crowds as we see happening today.

This was the early 1970s, long before the popular worship music phenomenon would sweep the globe. My public experience up to that point had been pretty much limited to singing in the youth choir in my traditional Full Gospel church. Singing solos or leading songs in front of people petrified me. That day in my bedroom I was simply lifting my voice to the Lord at full throttle, enjoying fellowship with Him while listening to a vinyl record of Sammy Hall singing "Bridge Over Troubled Water." He sang it not like Simon & Garfunkel but as a gospel song, referring to Jesus as that bridge over troubled waters.

Coming from a loving, secure home, I had little comprehension at age thirteen of what troubled waters really meant for some people. But connecting intimately with the Lord through worship was becoming my refuge and source of strength, and it would become a lifeline in the years to come. I would indeed have some very deep troubled waters to cross, and Jesus would be my bridge.

Worshipping in both the difficult and the pleasant moments of life takes us to a place of peace and stillness with the Father as nothing else does. In many ways that has been the story of my life. Music moves me. In everything I see, touch, hear, or experience, I can almost always sense a song wanting to break forth. It also seems fitting that I was singing "Bridge Over Troubled Water" when the vision occurred. Helping people draw a little closer to Jesus, especially when going through their own turbulent storms, has since become core to my calling. I've always been drawn to songs that give hope and encouragement.

I believe the vision I had that day was prophetic because over the years, the Lord has allowed me to lead thousands in worship, just as I saw in the vision. It wasn't planned or manipulated but unfolded as the Holy Spirit led. When I married Marcus, I had no clue what the future would hold; I saw only what was immediately before us. While we were called to start a Christian television station in Montgomery, Alabama, and certainly had a big vision, I don't think anyone could have foreseen just how far God would take us—from using thrown-away equipment dug out of a dumpster in a small TV market to the Daystar Television Network broadcasting in every country in the world. We were simply two kids obeying the Lord one step at a time.

Joni Lamb & the Daystar Singers and Band would play an important role. Our worship music has gone around the globe, and we lead worship in front of the whole world every day. What's crazy is when I married Marcus, I didn't sing solos; I couldn't even sit in front of people without my stomach being in knots. And as I said, my singing experience had pretty much been limited to the choir, my room, and my car.

It was Marcus who saw something in me and pushed me to develop my gift. And he would always be the one behind me saying, "You can do this. I hear you singing in the other room, and you need to develop that gift." I can look back and see so many times in my life when he encouraged me. And he saw things I didn't see. But what you have to understand, and what is critical to this chapter, is that whether I recorded music projects or not, worship was foundational in my life. I'm drawn to worship that's intimate, where you are talking to the Father as you sing.

From the onset, almost all my music projects have been centered around worship. In the beginning I was the only singer. Later, Bobby Binion joined me, and eventually Joe Ninowski came and helped me form the Daystar Singers and Band. Between my solo projects and the ones with the Daystar Singers, we have produced around fifteen albums. Occasionally I will sing a solo, but if you watch Joni Lamb & the Daystar Singers and Band on television or listen to our CDs, you'll see that primarily I'm part of a group worshipping. Why is this important? It's important because I am a worshipper at heart, and there's something about worshipping the Lord in the midst of our storms that brings us into alignment with Him.

GOD SHOWS UP WHEN WE WORSHIP

A couple of years ago, our group released a single featuring Michael Bethany titled "Peace Be Still," and it struck a chord with listeners worldwide. One of the stanzas says this:

> Your power (Your power)
> Is my peace (Is my peace)
> You are my healing (Your healing)
> All that I need (All that I need)
> Through the fire (Through the fire)
> Even in the storm (In the storm)
> Beyond (Beyond all understanding)
> You are my peace.[1]

We can have peace and stillness when the waves get rough. When it comes to rising above our storms, worship is vital. There's no greater act of faith than worshipping God when we are hurting. Actually, it's impossible to truly worship God in the midst of painful situations unless you're walking in faith. There is a vast difference between worshipping and singing. The act of worship actually ignites faith and moves the hand of God. I'm not talking about singing a song about God. I'm talking about creating intimacy with the Father by praising

Him and acknowledging who He is right in the middle of your chaos and pain, when your situation looks hopeless.

I recorded the song "Peacespeaker" nearly thirty years ago. It was written by my good friend Geron Davis. The lyrics are embedded in my spirit even today.

> It was such a lovely day
> And the sun was shining bright
> The gentle winds were blowing my way
> Not a storm cloud was in sight
> Then suddenly without warning
> A storm surrounds my life
> But even in the storm,
> I could feel the calm
> And here's the reason why
>
> I know the Peacespeaker
> I know Him by name
> I know the Peacespeaker
> He controls the wind and the waves
> When He says, Peace be still
> They have to obey
> I know the Peacespeaker
> Yes I know Him by name.
>
> There's never been another name
> With the power of this friend
> By simply saying, Peace be still
> He can calm the strongest wind
> That's why I never worry
> When storm clouds come my way
> I know that He is near

To drive away my fear
And I can smile and say

I know the Peacespeaker
I know Him by name
I know the Peacespeaker
He controls the wind and the waves.[2]

Worship is God's way. When we worship in the midst of our storm, God shows up. I love the story of Paul and Silas in the Bible. You probably know it too, but I want you to fully grasp what's going on here. First we need to read Acts 16:22–26 (emphasis added):

> Then the multitude rose up together against them; and the magistrates tore off their [Paul's and Silas'] clothes and commanded them to be beaten with rods. And when they had laid many stripes on them, they threw them into prison, commanding the jailer to keep them securely. Having received such a charge, he put them into *the inner prison and fastened their feet in the stocks.* But at midnight Paul and Silas *were praying and singing hymns to God,* and the prisoners were listening to them. Suddenly there was a great earthquake, so that the foundations of the prison were shaken; and immediately all the doors were opened and everyone's chains were loosed.

Think about it. Paul and Silas were beaten with rods and had many stripes laid on them. Their flesh was slashed, bruised, and bleeding. Open to the elements, their wounds were oozing and stinging. The men were in physical agony. Then they were thrown into the inner prison. This was the deepest, darkest, coldest dungeon—the absolute worst and most secure place. On top of that their feet were clasped in wooden stocks that locked so they couldn't move. It was incredibly uncomfortable, and being uncomfortable is difficult. There were probably rats scurrying around in the darkness, perhaps crawling across their feet and legs. Can you imagine what the prison must have been like? It was not a pretty sight.

Paul and Silas were not telling each other, "Hey, don't worry; just be happy. We'll be outa here soon and home for dinner." No, just the opposite. They figured they would be there a while and were likely to die. Seeing Christians martyred was something Paul was accustomed to. And don't forget the raw, physical pain they were in.

I would say what Paul and Silas were experiencing definitely qualified as a storm. It would have been enough to make most of us ball up our fists and cry out, "Why me, God? How could You allow this?" Job did that. He cried out, "Why, God?" But God could handle it, and He answered. Job didn't sin, because even though he had questions, he knew that despite his conditions his Redeemer lived (Job 19:25). It's OK if you have questions for God when you're going through deep and troubled waters. He's a big God and can handle it.

Yet what happened with Paul and Silas? At midnight they were "praying and singing hymns to God" (Acts 16:25). Those words "to God" mean they were worshipping intimately. The Amplified Bible says they were "singing hymns of praise to God." The New Life Version says they were "singing songs of thanks to God." No matter which Bible translation you read, the question remains: How do you do that? How do you thank God sincerely when you are being tortured and facing death? You have to know He is present and that something bigger is going on. Paul and Silas understood the reality that Jesus had risen from the dead and was right there with them through the Holy Spirit, regardless of their feelings and the horrific circumstances. None of their hardships destroyed their faith in the Lord.

Worshipping the Lord during our storms is faith in action. It has nothing to do with how well we sing or what we feel about our voices. Our worship is a "sacrifice of praise to God, that is, the fruit of our lips, giving thanks to His name" (Heb. 13:15). Giving a "sacrifice of praise" does not mean you praise God for horrible things such as getting beaten to shreds and thrown in prison, or having a diesel truck fall on you. We don't worship God because of our pain; we worship Him despite our pain. We worship Him for who He is. Like Paul and Silas, we praise God because we realize something bigger is going on.

Worship combined with prayer and confessing the Word of God equals intimacy. What was the result for Paul and Silas? God showed up in a miraculous way by sending an earthquake that shook the prison to its foundations. Chains were broken, and captives were set free; even the jailer was changed by God's power. The Lord wants to do that for all of us who are chained by strongholds and locked up in prisons of false freedom. I've never had my back beaten or been thrown into prison, but the enemy has definitely tried to take me out. As life became more intense during my personal storms, the Lord taught me how to praise my way through, and He has shown up again and again, even miraculously at times. If I'm in a bad place or struggling in some area, I pray and worship.

WORSHIP IS A WEAPON

Why is it important to worship during our trials? One reason is that there's a real enemy that wants to take us out, and worship is a weapon. Some storms are just natural issues of life, but other storms are direct attacks from the enemy. God wants to give us wisdom and discernment in those times. Charles Kraft, PhD, a prolific author and communications specialist, wrote in his book *Worship: Beyond the Hymnbook*: "Worship is one of the most important things human beings can do, not because it feeds God's ego but because it lines us up with him against our enemy, Satan. Worship is an act of war. It is also an act of participation, strengthening our relationship with God and with each other....In worship we declare that we are on God's side. We declare this to God, to ourselves, to other people, and to the spirit realm."[3]

From the moment Marcus and I said yes to God, the enemy tried to distract, derail, and kill us, because whenever something is of God, the enemy always tries to kill it at its conception. It was 1986, and I had just finished recording my first album, which had gospel songs and a worship medley. Our son, Jonathan, was nine months old, and I left him with his daddy while I drove up to Kentucky with a girlfriend to record. It was roughly an eight-hour drive each way, and we were at the end of our trip. I had dropped my friend off and was only a couple of miles from my house.

The whole time I drove, I listened to the song "The Blood Bought Church," which I had just recorded. The song is rousing and triumphant, reminding us that we are in the army of the Lord and nothing can stop us because we're a mighty force! It was cranked up loud, and I was rocking as I cruised down the highway. Out of my peripheral vision I noticed a car coming up on the right. There was an intersection, but I had the green light, so I was moving forward because I thought the driver was going to stop at the red light. I continued toward the intersection, probably going sixty or sixty-five miles per hour, and the other car continued forward too! By the time I realized he wasn't going to stop, I was entering the intersection.

The other driver was now in the middle of the intersection, and I slammed on my brakes and swerved right to avoid hitting him head-on, which would have killed one or both of us. My car struck his back end. As it did, I thought, "I'm going to die. I have no way to stop this." Everything was happening so fast, yet it seemed as if I were moving in slow motion. In those seconds, I heard the Lord say, "No, you're not." And then I felt two invisible arms come around me and hold me secure. I didn't have a seat belt on, and those arms wrapped around me from behind and held me. I know it may sound impossible, but that really happened.

The impact totaled my car; I actually jumped out because I thought it was going to explode like in the movies. As I walked away, I could still hear "Blood Bought Church" playing in the background. The police came, and then Marcus. It was determined the guy driving the other vehicle was drunk. He was banged up pretty bad, but the outcome could have been much different. If I hadn't swerved, neither of us would be here. The Lord totally showed up for me, wrapping me in His arms. I believe worshipping God brings a manifestation of His presence, and that's what miraculously happened that day. Even before I knew a storm was brewing, God was with me, preserving me as I worshipped.

STEPS THROUGH THE STORM

> Fear not, for I am with you; be not dismayed, for I am your God. I will strengthen you, yes, I will help you, I will *uphold* [support] you with My righteous right hand.
>
> —ISAIAH 41:10, EMPHASIS ADDED

When we get weary from a long day of work or play, many of us love coming home and crashing in our favorite recliner. When we drop, we have absolute faith that the chair is going to support, or *uphold,* us. We're so confident that we don't even think about it. The Lord is sturdier than any recliner. When you have the same kind of faith in His promises, you can crash in the "chair" of His loving arms and just be still. Sitting in His presence allows you to worship Him in the storm. When you have no idea what to pray or which scripture to read, just begin to worship Him. Soon you will be taken into His presence.

Psalm 34:1–4 says, "I will extol the LORD at all times; his praise will always be on my lips. I will glory in the LORD; let the afflicted hear and rejoice. Glorify the LORD with me; let us exalt his name together. I sought the LORD, and he answered me; he delivered me from all my fears" (NIV). May that also be our prayer.

> *Lord, by faith I offer the sacrifice of praise to You in the midst of my circumstances. I choose to believe You are in control, and I trust You to*

uphold me. You are delivering me from all my fears as I worship Your mighty name. Amen.

Chapter 5

SNAKEBITES

THERE'S THE SEVEN-YEAR tribulation period spoken of in the Book of Revelation, and then there are the seven years we spent in Montgomery, Alabama. I don't know if the two tribulation periods are the same, but I could make a strong argument for it! Of course I'm being facetious, but there were times in Montgomery when it felt like pure tribulation. Sometimes, as we saw earlier, God calls us into the storm, and then the storm intensifies when we are there. God called us to Montgomery. In reality, though, the Lord was preparing us for another great move that would launch us to a whole different level. Along the way, there would be a myriad of storms, but as you'll see, the Lord was there guiding, delivering, and confirming. The enemy was there too, still trying to take us out.

One of the truths I've learned is that not only does the Lord often use our storms as vehicles to get us to our ultimate destination; He will also use them to minister through us along the way. If you are in a battering storm right now, don't think that God can't use you. Actually, it's the exact opposite. There are people in the midst of the turbulence with you who need to hear your message of hope. Right now I'm thinking of two precious saints of God. One has to go to the cancer center for regular chemotherapy treatment. The other has to get dialysis for kidney failure. While at their respective medical facilities, they sit for hours among others receiving treatment. Both are believing God for their healings, but in the process God is using them powerfully to bring the light of Jesus to those they interact with while getting treatment.

I've heard story after story of how the Lord has used a person to encourage someone who had lost hope. Once more I'm reminded of the apostle Paul. At another point in his life he was imprisoned yet again, thinking the end of his earthly life was near. While sitting there in chains, he wrote these astounding words to the church at Philippi:

> But I want you to know, brethren, that the things which happened to me have actually turned out for the furtherance of the gospel, so that it has become evident to the whole palace guard, and to all the rest, that my chains are in Christ.
>
> —PHILIPPIANS 1:12–13

Can you believe God was so interested in the souls of the palace guard and "all the rest" that He allowed Paul to be imprisoned so he could be a light in their darkness? Paul was not complaining about his situation, and it wasn't a lack of faith that put him there. Again, he recognized that the Lord was right there with him, using him despite his difficult circumstances.

On still another occasion, Paul had set sail for Rome. He knew he was called to go there and minister. God, however, allowed his method of transportation to be a prison ship carrying more than 250 convicts, with Paul chained as one of them. If that's not bad enough, a massive nor'easter hit and tossed the ship around like a rag doll, driving it off course. All the prisoners thought they were going to die, but the Lord was right there with Paul in the midst of the storm. Paul told the prisoners:

> I urge you [men] to keep up your *courage*, because not one of you will be lost; only the ship will be destroyed. Last night an angel of the God to whom I belong and whom I serve stood beside me and said, "Do not be afraid, Paul. You must stand trial before Caesar; and God has graciously given you the lives of all who sail with you." So keep up your courage, men, for I have faith in God that it will happen just as he told me. Nevertheless, we must run aground on some island.
> —ACTS 27:22–26, NIV, EMPHASIS ADDED

It seems there are a lot of neverthelesses in our lives that the Lord uses. The ship ran aground on the island of Malta, which had friendly inhabitants who welcomed the men with open arms. It was cold and raining on the beach, so the men built a fire to warm themselves. Paul picked up a pile of sticks, and then a poisonous viper jumped out and latched on to his hand. Paul simply shook the serpent off and carried on with his business, never missing a beat. The other people were standing around, waiting for Paul to drop dead. They were sure this attack happened because of some grievous sin in his life that upset the gods. (Sounds like many religious people I know!)

But when Paul didn't keel over, the other men changed their tune. They then thought he was a god and wanted to worship him. Paul assured them that he was no god, but he did know the one true God. They listened and then took him to the chief official of the island, whose father was sick and near death. Paul wound up praying for him, and the man was miraculously healed. "When this was done," Luke wrote, "the rest of those on the island who had diseases also came and were healed" (Acts 28:9). Revival broke out on the island of Malta. Paul and his gang of prisoners stayed there for three months during the winter, and Paul continued to minister God's love and grace. Eventually the Lord provided a different ship that had wintered on the island, and it was time to move on, so they set sail to Rome.

My question to you is this: What are you doing in your storm?

OUR PERSONAL MALTA

Marcus and I knew we were called to Montgomery to build WMCF at TV-45. It would be a learning and practice season. We just didn't know for how long. Marcus told me, "I know we were supposed to come here, but I know this isn't where we're supposed to stay." We knew we would be moving on eventually. In many ways Montgomery was like a place where we were shipwrecked. Marcus still did some evangelistic events because we had little income, but God faithfully showed up for us again and again. We started building by faith. Again, who teaches you how to build a television station? But we had a word from God to do it. If He called us to do it, He would see us through it. He was our source and our director. We had a mandate to build the station, get it on the air, and use it to preach the gospel. God told us to do it, and we had a peace about doing it, but it wasn't easy.

Montgomery was our Malta, and there would be some snakes that would bite and try to stop us. However, by God's grace and power we would shake them off and keep moving forward. Ministry would go forth. When we first built the station, we were on a short tower. If you're on a short tower, the signal's not going as far. You're not able to reach as many people. The taller your tower, the better. It's common sense, right? That's why you see so many towers up on mountains; the higher you go, the broader your coverage.

We eventually got an opportunity to transmit from a much taller tower. It was eight hundred feet, and the tower we were on was three hundred feet, so this would be a huge improvement, and we'd reach so many more people. Marcus negotiated a deal with the radio station building the tower allowing us to lease space on it and place our antenna at the top, thereby enabling us to reach more people.

One night I went to sleep like normal and had a dream. In my dream I saw that tower going up, and I saw them taking our transmission line up the tower, and then they started pulling it down really fast. I remember saying in the dream, "No, you can't do that. We've got to go on this tower. We've got to reach more people." The dream was so vivid that I woke Marcus up and told him about it. He said, "Oh, honey, everything's fine on the tower."

I felt very disturbed by the dream because it seemed as if it were in living color. I couldn't go back to sleep, so I got up and started pacing in the living room. I didn't know what to pray, so I just said, "Lord, I don't know what this is, but I'm thanking You in advance that You're going to work all this out." After that, I prayed in the Spirit. A wave of peace about the tower came over me, and I went back to bed. Within the next two days, Marcus got a call from the people building the tower. They said, "Oh, we decided not to let you go on this tower."

Marcus came to me and said, "Tell me about that dream again." So I told him what I'd seen.

"What did you do?" Marcus asked.

"I just got up and prayed," I told him.

"Well, thank God for that," he said. Then he went to battle as he always did and told them all the reasons they had to keep the deal. The bottom line is that we ended up getting on the tower. Remember, the first time we built the station, it was pretty pitiful. Eventually we were able to get on the taller tower. We got a better transmitter, a better antenna, and a new transmission line, all of which gave us better coverage for the city of Montgomery. I believe in prophecy and that God will let His servants know things. During the ensuing decades, the Holy Spirit guided and directed me with undeniable confirmation.

Whenever someone flips on the television and sees *Table Talk* or *Ministry Now* or any of the other anointed programs on Daystar, they see where we are now. It's difficult for many to wrap their minds around what God brought us through to get to this point. It's hard for me to wrap my own mind around it. I'm just a girl from Greenville, South Carolina. I'm just a regular Joe. I have struggles and wrestle with things. This book is not about me doing all the right things and God blessing me—not at all. However, I hope my story shows you that God can use anybody who's willing to take His hand and He will do amazing things despite their weaknesses and failings.

The enemy wanted to destroy us because he knew what God could do and the global impact we could have. As I'm writing this chapter, Daystar is in 2.2 billion homes worldwide and in every country in the world. We've seen hundreds of thousands of people saved. I'm talking about people who were lost and going to hell giving their hearts to Jesus. In just one revival crusade that Marcus led, forty-four hundred people accepted the Lord and signed salvation cards. The only reason I'm saying all this is to boast in the Lord. Paul the apostle did not hold back when he boasted about what God had done. My point is, God brought us through decades of one storm after another. He gave us divine dreams and guidance. He'll do the same thing in your life. It's just that we are all on different journeys.

Just as I didn't sing solos, I also didn't talk in front of large groups. I had no idea I would minister in that way until we built the station in Montgomery and Marcus said, "I need you to sit up there with me."

I told him, "Oh, no. I'm not talking. I don't know what to say. I don't have a degree in theology like you do."

He said, "No, it's just that there are more women who watch, and you need to be here with me."

So I did it. I went and sat with Marcus, but my stomach was in knots. Every night, we would go on for two hours, seven to nine, Monday through Friday. But after a couple of months of my stomach being all knotted up every night, I was getting ready to go to the show and said, "Lord, I can't do this."

I sensed the Holy Spirit say, "I'll tell you what, I'll make a deal with you. You go on and be yourself, and I'll go with you and tell you what to say."

I thought, "OK. Deal."

So that's what I started doing, and that's what I've been doing ever since. Although it's pretty natural now and I'm comfortable talking, it didn't begin that way. That's because ministering on television is a gift God gave me that I didn't know was in there. It was a gift that had to be developed.

It's funny when I think about it. In the beginning I wouldn't say anything until Marcus started talking. By the time we got to Dallas, I was talking more than he was in the interviews that we did together. I was supposed to be Marcus' cohost, but I was tapping him to say, "I've got a question. I've got a question." Finally he said, "You need your own show. You're good at interviewing people, and you like listening to people's stories, so you need your own show." He was the one who pushed me to host my own program. It was definitely a God thing that brought me to that point.

The show was first called *Taking a Break With Joni*. Then we called it *The Joni Show*, and under that name the National Religious Broadcasters named it the Best Television Talk Show in 2004. The show later grew into what became *Joni Table Talk*. In the past year we've been airing daily on A&E and FYI, networks, as well as on CBS and Fox Business on the weekends. What God is doing is way bigger than this girl.

God has us in the right place at the right time for His good purposes, and He has equipped us to do the work He sets before us to do. Through the process God has shown me things about myself—things that were in me that I had not seen or known. I can look back and see that through the storms and snakebites, God had a master plan. He was guiding and preparing us for what was coming. Ask the Lord to show you the gift He's put in you, and let Him develop it. It may surprise you. All you have to do is surrender all and be obedient. He will do the rest.

STEPS THROUGH THE STORM

> Yet who knows whether you have come to the kingdom for such a time as this?
> —ESTHER 4:14

When the enemy's poisonous snakes fasten their fangs onto you, just shake them off as Paul did and keep moving forward. Snakes can be people who try to discredit you or slander you, or who betrayed you. Snakes can be personal failures or mistakes. Even though it hurts at the moment of the strike, you can't afford to let the venom of bitterness or self-pity poison your life.

God has plans for you. He has an assignment for you right in the place where you are. When the enemy tells you that you are purposeless, God says you were created with purpose. In fact, perhaps this is the moment for which you were created. Don't give up, and don't give in! Shake off that snake and keep going. Even if you can't see it, what you are doing now has an eternal impact on you and those around you.

Lord, empower me to simply shake off the enemy's snakes when they latch on to my life so I can keep moving forward with my assignment. You created me with unique gifts and abilities for this very moment. Help me see that Your purpose is in the small things and be a light to those watching around me. Amen.

Chapter 6

STAYING IN THE SUPERNATURAL

A T THE CHRIST For The Nations Institute on June 26, 1996, Bible teacher Marilyn Hickey spoke a prophetic word over Marcus and me. She charged us to "stay in the supernatural." But what in the world did she mean by that? Well, to start, you have to already be *in* something to *stay in* it. We were moving in the supernatural, and Marilyn was encouraging us to never step out of that lane. There's no other way to explain how this ministry grew from the seed the Lord planted in our hearts to where we are now than to say it was supernatural.

Though we had to choose to follow the Holy Spirit's leading, Daystar's impact has been a sovereign work of God. The vision was way bigger than Marcus, and it's way bigger than me. Undeniably, Marcus was a special, anointed vessel, handpicked by the Lord. We both were, and we both took some pretty devastating blows that in the natural should have shattered us. But the Lord held us together, cracks and all. Fortunately for us, He loves to shine His light through our cracks. In fact, cracked vessels with light emanating from inside them are beautiful, prized works of art. That could be one way to define the ministry the Lord has given us: just be real and let His light shine through the cracks in your life.

On November 15, 1996, five months after Marilyn Hickey gave us that word, another world-renowned minister, whom I'll keep nameless, prophesied that God would give our fledgling television ministry a whole network of TV stations and that if we would never be ashamed of the Holy Spirit and would always stand for revival, our ministry would go around the world. That was unheard of and seemed impossible. It was a bold and risky prophecy that could have ruined this minister's credibility if it wasn't accurate. But a little over a year later, the Lord miraculously opened the door for Daystar to acquire several new TV stations and become a national TV network.

From that moment on it was like a stream of dominoes falling as we began to acquire TV station after TV station in city after city across America, allowing us to blanket the nation with the much-needed message of the gospel. The reports of lives being changed were staggering.

Then the dominoes just kept falling as Daystar went global in Africa, Europe, the Middle East, Central and South America, Australia, New Zealand, and India. Countries such as the United Arab Emirates (Dubai), the Virgin Islands, Nepal, the United Kingdom, Pakistan, the Philippines, Scandinavia and the Baltic States, Israel, Germany, Belgium, the Netherlands, and Italy were receiving Daystar programming—and the list is still growing. As of 2023 *Joni Table Talk* is on other networks, including CBS, A&E, FYI network, and Fox Business. It's not a stretch to say Daystar is reaching *billions* of souls with a message of hope and healing.

All this started with two young kids who didn't know much

or have much but sought to hear the voice of the Holy Spirit and follow Him. Sometimes obedience meant making sacrifices and trusting God when we didn't fully understand what He was up to. And when we would simply obey in faith, He would supernaturally bring us through and entrust us with more.

When God called us to Dallas after those seven years in Montgomery, Marcus and I had to start over again from scratch. In December of 1990, we moved into a little apartment in Euless, Texas, close to the Dallas-Fort Worth airport with Jonathan, who was almost five, and eleven-month-old Rachel. Rebecca would come soon after, in 1992. It was not easy juggling family life in a small space along with the growing demands of the ministry. It was a walk of faith. But we eventually moved into a small three-bedroom home before Rebecca was born, and I was so thankful.

Here's something most people who watch Daystar these days probably don't know—especially the critics: when Marcus and I were preparing to move to Dallas, we got an offer from a secular businessman to sell the station in Montgomery for almost three million dollars. In the natural it seemed like the favor of God. Do you know what three million dollars would have done for us? It would have set us up to basically buy and build the station in Dallas. Yet God had another plan. He wanted to keep us living in faith.

Just as the Holy Spirit "forbade" the apostle Paul from going into certain regions in Acts 16, the Holy Spirit forbade us from selling, even when it appeared the right thing to do. He wanted the station to remain dedicated to Christian ministry. Although the businessman was honorable, we had to turn him down and give it to God, and the station in Montgomery remains Christian to this day.

Consider that again. We turned down three million dollars. In addition, Marcus sold the five acres of land his parents had gifted him as a college graduation present to come up with the $10,000 earnest money needed for the construction permit to build a TV station in Dallas. In so many ways we could have justified selling and taking the three million dollars, but the Lord said no. Talk about a step of faith!

Here's what I'm not saying: I'm not saying we didn't make mistakes. We made plenty. We're not all that. It's worth repeating that this has been a supernatural, sovereign work of God beyond anything Marcus and I could have accomplished ourselves. We were, and still are, merely stewards of what the Lord is doing.

Of course the enemy, working through people and companies, wasn't too happy about what God was doing. Like a continuous bombardment of flaming arrows, one after another they would come against us. We faced lawsuits to keep us from expanding, buying new stations, getting licenses, building a tower—you name it. Lightning hit a tower, taking a station off the air for a while. Christian companies and leaders expressed doubt about our future and tried to discourage us from moving forward with building. We dealt with jealousy, false and misleading information being said and printed about us, the tower workers falling—I could go on and on.

As I said, we've had more than forty lawsuits filed against us and have never lost a single one—not one. God defends us. That doesn't keep the enemy from trying, though. This is yet another example of how obeying God can lead you into the storm so you can watch Him walk on the water, hold out His hand, and calm the turbulent waves. We were learning to sleep on the boat with Jesus while the lightning, thunder, and rain raged all around, threatening to sink us.

I use the word *supernatural* because that's really the only way to describe it. The Lord shows up outside the natural realm to speak, guide, protect, and provide. I strongly believe in the supernatural because of the undeniable things I've seen God do for us. Those arms that wrapped around me in the car crash that night were real. I'm not exaggerating. The prophetic dream about our equipment being torn down from the tower was real. I couldn't know that was going to happen. But the dream showed us what they would try and how to pray. I really did hear the Lord call my name audibly three times, as I shared in the preface. There are so many of these divine instances, and we're going to see more of the personal ones later in the book.

Daystar is also committed to staying in the supernatural in our programming. The myriad of credible, undeniable, documented testimonies from people I've been privileged to interview only strengthen my resolve and faith. Our hope is that they strengthen yours too.

Amy Keesee Freudiger is a woman we interviewed on *Table Talk* who had a thirteen-pound tumor in her abdomen. The tumor caused a curvature of her spine and made her look as if she were pregnant. Amy is a beautiful, glowing woman filled with the presence of God, yet for years people who didn't know her thought she was pregnant. For various reasons, the doctors couldn't or wouldn't perform surgery. Her condition was humiliating, embarrassing, and painful, and self-hatred stalked her. I'd say this qualified as a turbulent storm.

Amy, however, decided to go to a higher source than her doctors. She went on a thirty-day dare and shut herself off from voices of fear, death, and destruction, including those coming through TV, radio, magazines, and other reading material. For that period, she spoke healing scriptures out loud three times a day. Amy says, "I was determined to flood every cell of my body with Truth."[1] But her body didn't change, and it seemed she was making declarations to the walls and ceiling. Yet Amy refused to give up.

One day during prayer at church, the Holy Spirit overwhelmed Amy with heat, and something that felt like warm oil flowed through her body. Amy knew instantly that she was healed. The Holy Spirit affirmed to her spirit that her healing had occurred. But still nothing happened physically; her body was as disfigured as it ever was. Two weeks later Amy was being fitted for a bridesmaid outfit, and the woman fitting her asked if she was pregnant. Amy was once again devastated. Her waist was measured, and that night right before bed she stepped on the scale and weighed herself.

The next morning when Amy woke up, her stomach felt sore, as if she had worked out. Her husband, lying beside her, peeked out from the covers. When he saw his wife, his eyes became like saucers. "Amy, look at your stomach!" he cried out. The thirteen-pound tumor that had been there for years had disappeared overnight! It was completely gone. Amy's belly button, which had become an outie, was now a perfectly formed innie. Amy had lost nine inches from her waist and thirteen pounds overnight! The doctors were baffled. There are before-and-after pictures to prove it. In one picture Amy looks like a pregnant woman; in the next she looks like a fitness instructor. The old X-ray shows the curved spine; the new one shows her spine is straight.[2]

Amy's healing took place long before the physical manifestation occurred. Honestly, I don't understand why some people are healed and others aren't, but it's undeniable that Amy experienced a supernatural miracle. You can read her full story in her book *Healed Overnight.* I've interviewed so many others who have had divine encounters and received miracles. We are committed to staying in biblical truth and in the legitimate, documented supernatural, just as Marilyn said.

A MIRACULOUS OPPORTUNITY

Getting back to Daystar, there were so many God things that happened each step of the way that confirmed where we were going. I could write a whole book just on Daystar. That's not what this book is about, but I had to lay a foundation so you would know where God brought us from and what He brought us through. This chapter is transitional and critical before I get into some of my darker, more personal storms. However, I would be remiss if I did not tell you this next supernatural story of how God made a way for Daystar's home base.

When Marcus felt God calling us to the Dallas-Fort Worth (DFW) metroplex, he understood that it was a top-ten market for television, a massive market that costs millions of dollars to reach. But Marcus was all about reaching more people with the gospel. There were corporations clamoring to be on the air in Dallas with limited availability. Corporations threw millions of dollars around like they were one-dollar bills to broadcast in this top-ten market. How in the world could a young couple with nothing even hope to build something here? The whole idea would have been absolutely insane unless the God of the supernatural was involved, the God who delights in making a way where it seems there is no way. He's a God who delights in shutting the mouths of lions, parting seas, and using young boys to slay giants.

An opportunity to buy a construction permit to build a TV station outside DFW became available. The problem was that it was licensed in the city of Decatur, Texas, which is approximately fifty miles outside the Dallas-Fort Worth metroplex. For some reason, the permit had been obtained but the station had never been built. In television the Federal Communications Commission (FCC) requires you to put what it calls a "city-grade" signal over your city of license. That means if you build a station in Decatur, you're not going to reach the Dallas-Fort Worth metroplex. You're going to reach only a small portion of it. You're not going to cover the main population.

None of the big players in television wanted the permit. But the Lord moved on Marcus to get the topographical maps and study them again. He started in Dallas and lined the pins out to Decatur. It showed a steady incline, and Decatur was up on a hill. Well, in television, the line of sight is everything. So Marcus and our engineer—who, by the way, is still with us— did something that had never been done before: they physically went on location and did what they call a signal strength measurement. What they discovered is they could put a tower in Dallas, and because Decatur is up on a hill, the line of sight from the Dallas-Fort Worth TV tower and transmitter would carry a city-grade signal over Decatur while still covering the entire Dallas-Fort Worth metroplex.

The whole time they were realizing this, Marcus was thinking, "Could this be real, Lord? How can the big guys not see this?" It was like a little hidden diamond in the rough up there—actually, a big precious diamond! Because of this discovery, the FCC changed the rules for us, something that had never been done. We were able to put up our tower in Dallas, the very same tower the workers fell off, and then we would have a television station that would reach millions and be worth millions more just because it is in the top-ten market.

After we bought the rights and permits, a lawsuit was filed against us when the sellers realized they could have had an effective tower in Dallas. They knew then that the permit was worth a lot more money. So they came back and said, "This wasn't right. You didn't pay us enough money." But that was because they hadn't done their due diligence and hadn't figured it out. They got really upset when they realized, "Oh my goodness, we've sold this permit, and look what they've done with it." But that was just the Lord giving us favor. My point is that the potential of that permit was hidden all those years. So many people would have grabbed the permit if they realized it could be used in this bigger market, but the tower wasn't built until we came. It was for such a time as this.

We have an administrative, business side like all Christian organizations, but the core vision has not changed—reaching lost and hurting people with the gospel and sharing stories of hope. The next twenty-something years were a blur, as God took us from nowhere to around the globe. That season was wonderful and brutal, rewarding and devastating. As it is with pastors, juggling home life and ministry is challenging. There were times when our flesh was tired, but quitting wasn't an option. Growing Daystar was a fight—a war, really. But God would work miracles that would keep us going.

How is all of this relevant to your life? Each of us is on a different journey, but the principles are the same. Often we think we are writing a book with our lives, but God is using the process to write us. In July of 2003, Marcus celebrated thirty years in ministry. The enemy couldn't shut us down, but the roughest storm lay ahead.

STEPS THROUGH THE STORM

My speech and my preaching was not with enticing words of man's wisdom, but in demonstration of the Spirit and of power, so that your faith should not stand in the wisdom of men, but in the power of God.

—1 CORINTHIANS 2:4–5, MEV

The Lord wants to show up supernaturally in your life, just as He has done in mine. It takes the supernatural to walk through the storms. You can only survive the tempest when the Lord comes to you on the waves and calls you to walk out on the water with Him. There's no way you can pull it off in your own power. The storm is way bigger than you. But God promises to show up! If you are sensitive to the Holy Spirit's voice, He will speak to you personally about every situation you face and give you specific steps to take. "Your faith should not stand in the wisdom of men, but in the power of God" (1 Cor. 2:5, MEV). The Lord is going to see you through supernaturally. He's going to show up in demonstrations of His Spirit, and what He does will be a testimony of His power, not yours.

> *Lord, Your Word is a lamp to my feet and a light to my path. I believe You are supernaturally guiding me by Your Holy Spirit. Help me tune in to Your voice and obey. Amen.*

Chapter 7

WORTH FIGHTING FOR

I CAN REMEMBER EXACTLY what I was wearing the day I found out. I had interviewed journalist Deborah Norville about her new book and was still in the studio when my parents called. That's a funny thing about trauma; you can remember every detail of that day. But you know you are healed from it when years later you can recount the story and not feel the pain associated with it. I have experienced so much healing in my life, which is why I can write about this now.

What happened that day reminds me of the first time I visited the Sea of Galilee in Israel. Our tour guide explained how quickly storms can blow in. When the boat leaves the shore, the sky can be as clear as crystal and the water as smooth as glass, but then, seemingly out of nowhere, dark clouds blow in, unleashing a raging tempest that rocks the ship. As I gazed out over the placid water, I couldn't imagine a storm suddenly sweeping in. The tour guide's statement seemed unreal to me, but it's true nonetheless. I think the reality is, life can be like that too. Everything can be calm and quiet, the sun can be shining, and things can appear great. Then, just like that, a dark cloud blows in, the wind starts whipping, thunder and lightning crash, rain begins pouring down, and suddenly you find yourself being tossed on the waves, thinking your ship might sink.

That's what it was like for me that day in 2007. I wouldn't say life was as smooth as a sea of glass, but it was good. God was doing great things in our family and at Daystar. As you can imagine, though, Marcus and I were doing life at a pretty brisk pace that often had us running in different directions. In the middle of this busyness my parents called, saying I needed to come to their house immediately because there was something urgent they needed to show me. They were working for us at the time, so I dropped everything and rushed over. The whole time I was driving, I was thinking, "What in the world do they have to show me that's so urgent?"

When I walked in, I could tell they had been crying, so I braced myself. Nothing, however, could have prepared me for what they presented to me. The pace of my life came to an abrupt halt. My heart sank, and a hollowness formed in the pit of my stomach as I read the revealing emails my dad had been given for me to see. Mom and Dad lived only a couple of miles from us, so I stayed at their house a moment to gain my composure as the severity of what I had discovered began to sink in. More like a bad dream than reality, it was hard for me to grasp that this was even happening. It couldn't be happening, not to us. Marcus was having an affair, and it was with a woman I thought was my friend.

When I finally made it home, the house was empty. Marcus was playing golf with a buddy of his. Jonathan was off at college. Rebecca and Rachel were busy with school, doing what high school girls do. So, I was there alone in the echoing silence. Our dream home now felt more like a brick-and-mortar shell.

As feelings of betrayal and anger rose inside me, one of my first thoughts was to lay out the emails so Marcus would find them one by one, like a fish being chummed. I'd watch him squirm and then just let him have it. That's what my flesh wanted to do. That's what my pain was screaming for me to do. But the Holy Spirit stopped me. Through the years I've come to recognize His loving, firm, comforting, warning voice. When I sense Him speaking—even faintly, beneath all the emotional noise—I try to pause and listen. That's not always easy to do. This time I did.

"OK, Lord. What do You want me to do?" I asked. After that, I prayed in the Spirit. Praying in the Spirit is something I learned early on when I was baptized in the Holy Spirit. It's one of our most powerful spiritual gifts, especially when we're in the midst of turbulence and don't know how to pray or what to do. Our own spirit within us groans, often through tears. Thankfully, tears are a language the Holy Spirit understands. It does us good to pause and pray in the Spirit before acting impulsively. "The Spirit helps us in our weakness. We do not know what we ought to pray for, but the Spirit himself intercedes for us through wordless groans" (Rom. 8:26, NIV).

This was me. As I was groaning in the Spirit, the Lord spoke clearly and unmistakably: "He's worth fighting for." Taken aback a bit by this revelation, I took a deep breath and then exhaled. *"He's worth fighting for."* This time a supernatural calmness filled me, and from that moment, the Lord surrounded me with what I call His Holy Spirit bubble. That's when Jesus, through His Spirit, protects you emotionally while He carries you. It's a spiritual version of walking on the waves. Really, that is the only way we can make it through devastating moments. Without His protective hand around our wounded hearts, we would shatter into a million pieces.

"OK, Lord. That's my directive," I said, resolving to follow His lead. And then I said, "Help me."

The Holy Spirit continued to lead me, saying, "Don't lay the emails out for him to find. Go put them in the room on your desk. Don't show him those. Go put them in there." I did that and went to change my clothes, but the Holy Spirit said, "Don't change. Stay just like you are."

"Yes, Lord," I answered. So I stayed dressed as I was and waited.

When Marcus finally made it home, he entered through the back door, calling out, "Tricks, are you here?" He called me Tricks because I liked to jump out and scare him sometimes and was always pulling tricks on him. He walked into the living room still wearing his golfing gear, smiling like he'd shot under par. "Hey, let's watch—" Marcus always had something he wanted us to watch together. But I interrupted him.

"I need to talk to you, Marcus," I said. "It's important." He sensed the seriousness in my tone and sat down. There was an awkward silence. I may have been trembling.

"What is it?" he asked.

"I know what's going on," I said.

A look of shock mixed with panic crossed his face. "What are you talking about?"

"I know about...," I answered, and I said her name. "I've seen the emails."

Marcus just dropped his head.

"How in the world could this happen to us?" I asked. Again,

what's amazing is that the Lord gave me supernatural, sustaining peace bigger than what was going on in the natural. You have to understand, I was one of those people who'd always said, "If he ever did that, I would divorce him in a heartbeat." But that's not what happened at all. I didn't condemn him or yell and scream; there was just a calm from the Lord. Now, later on I would yell and scream, but in that moment there was calmness. In my spirit I knew the Lord would navigate us through this storm.

"I'm so sorry," Marcus said. "I had no idea how to get out of this, and I was afraid to tell you."

We stayed up all night crying as I made Marcus recount every little detail, which was stupid. I wanted to know everything, and it was hard, but he told me everything. "I felt like I was on a roller coaster going a hundred miles per hour and I couldn't get off," he told me. "I felt like I was just barely hanging on and thought I would lose you if I told you. I'm glad it's all out." He sighed in anguish. "I'll do anything you want to make it right. I'm so sorry."

After everything was out in the open, the anger came, and I wanted to say words I never thought I'd say. I had to remind myself the Lord had said, "He's worth fighting for." And then I thought, "You know what? He *is* worth fighting for, and so is our marriage." We were going on twenty-five years; we had a wonderful family and a worldwide ministry. You'd better believe he was worth fighting for. Our marriage was worth fighting for. And if Marcus was saying, "I'll do anything, and I'm so sorry," then I could work with that. If he had said something like, "Well, I don't know how I feel about you. I don't know if I want to stay married," or that he loved her, that would have been another thing. But he didn't. He said, "I'm so sorry. I never wanted to hurt you." And you know what? I believed him.

"Well, we need to go to counseling," I said. And then Fred and Anna Kendall popped into my mind. I felt this was also direction from the Lord, and it would prove to be so. Located right here in Dallas, they are friends and are known internationally as experts in communication and relationships. These days Anna frequently sits at the table with me and the other ladies on *Table Talk*. Marcus and I didn't waste any time and went to see them the very next day. That was huge for Marcus. Many men resist counseling, but he humbled himself and said, "I'm listening and will follow." The Kendalls helped us plot a course for recovery.

SURRENDERING ALL

Meeting with the Kendalls was an act of faith on my part as well. I had to surrender my natural emotions that wanted to strike back. It's ironic because when all this happened, I had been working on my book *Surrender All*, and I had to surrender all during the writing process. The Lord consistently brings us to places of surrender, and storms are one of His methods of getting us there. Storms are opportunities to build altars of trust and faith to the Lord. Choosing to trust is an act of worship.

"Well, I guess we tell the world," I told Fred and Anna, because at that point we had a worldwide platform.

"No," Fred said. "You both are in intensive care. We're going to see if you can survive before we tell the world."

So for the next three years we worked on our relationship

and let ourselves heal. That first year of counseling and trying to stay together was excruciating. I wouldn't wish that on anybody. It was horrible having to go through the grueling process of recovery and reconciliation after that kind of breach, but we did it. We ultimately decided not to go public for those three years in order to protect our marriage. Only a handful of people knew what was going on—a couple of trusted people at Daystar, my mom and dad, and our accountability partners. Our kids didn't even know because we felt we needed to get well before we told them. At their ages, we didn't feel as if we needed to tell them. We knew we would; we just didn't know when that time would be.

I remember during counseling I would say over and over, "I can't believe this happened."

"Joni," Fred would say, "you don't live in Camelot. I know you think you do, but you don't."

And I really did think that. We'd had struggles and storms on the outside building Daystar, but I had never faced anything like this within my family. I guess I didn't believe it could happen to us. I mean, we were doing the Lord's work. How could it? And so, Camelot was shattered. And I realized this agony is what a lot of people have been through—maybe even you. If this is your story, don't give up hope that the Lord can give you His peace and direction on how to move forward. Learn to pray in the Spirit and listen to His promptings while the storm is beating down on you. He's real, alive, and fully present, and He sees.

This is not some pie-in-the-sky denial of reality. It *is* reality. Jesus through His Holy Spirit makes the difference in the storm. I don't want to suggest I've got it all together or to in any way deny the seriousness of the betrayal. That is not my intent at all. It's right to be angry and hurt when you go through something like this. But know that the Lord will show up for you, holding His hand out as we've talked about. When we take it, He is faithful to guide us to His best for us. God always has our best interests in mind. He won't force us to comply; He will change our hearts. That's what He did for me. He changed my heart. He healed my heart. I simply obeyed His instructions.

BETTER THAN BEFORE

Marcus and I had good days and bad days working through our issues—and there were many: broken trust, betrayal, heartache, anger, and so forth. But both of us were determined to rebuild better than before. It would take a miracle, but that's what the Lord does. One thing I had to do was let it go and quit talking about what had happened. Once I forgave, I couldn't keep reminding Marcus of his failure. We had to move past that. If we had an argument, I couldn't bring that back up. If we were going to stay together, I would have to let that go. You can't keep bringing up somebody's sin, reminding them of it; if you do, you'll destroy the relationship. "All have sinned and fall short of the glory of God," Paul wrote in Romans 3:23. That includes me. I knew I had to do the same thing for Marcus that the Lord had done for me.

I always knew Marcus loved me. That was never in doubt. During this process we'd have bad days, but the good ones were really good. The kids would ask, "What's happening to you and Dad? Why are y'all so lovey-dovey?" They had always known Marcus and I loved each other, but now there was more affection. We were more intentional with our marriage. When you almost lose something, you realize how precious it is. We both felt that way. Marcus could have lost me, and I could have lost him, and neither of us wanted that.

Looking back, I would say that next to Marcus dying, this was the most difficult storm I've ever gone through. It was the worst day of my life when I found out my sweetheart, the one God brought into my life, was having an affair. I couldn't believe it because anybody who knew Marcus knew he adored me. He had always been so good to me. So when I found out, I was understandably devastated. First came shock, then devastation, and then just hurt.

The big question was, How did we get to that place? How did we let something like that happen to us? Marcus and I never thought we'd find ourselves in that position. I knew I had been a good wife; I certainly wasn't a perfect one, but I knew I loved my husband. Through the counseling and recovery process, we identified a couple of key areas that had led Marcus into this trap.

One key was that the woman involved worked at Daystar, and part of her job required regular interaction with Marcus. They spent a lot of time talking on the phone. They became friends, and she started sharing personal information about her life, marriage, and so on. He would pray with her, and everything started very innocently. She found comfort in Marcus' kind heart and willingness to listen. I believe Marcus was naive and didn't realize where that kind of emotional connection could lead.

They also talked shop. This was at a time when Daystar's growth was exploding, and she was in a key position. She was an attractive, kindhearted, smart woman in a difficult marriage. Yes, I said "kindhearted" because she was likable, and I don't believe she set out to wreck our marriage. The affair unfolded. Their ongoing emotional connection continued to build until it morphed into something physical. And as already mentioned, she was my friend. Of all people. The betrayal from this kindhearted friend was like a knife twisting in my back. Later she would write a letter apologizing. I forgive her, and at the end of the day Marcus took full responsibility for his sin.

The second thing that led Marcus into that trap was that I was spending more time at the studio hosting my own show, which Marcus had encouraged me to do. I also hosted the show with him, did all the music, and oversaw production. There also were a lot of activities with the kids. Let's just say there was a lot of pressure on me. I'm not blaming myself. They made choices. Still, the Lord showed me that I could do better in many areas. And marriage should come first, always.

Marcus had been home with a bad cold and sinus infection. He later told me this was exactly when the door cracked opened just enough for the enemy to enter his mind. Marcus felt love through physical touch and words of affirmation. This woman provided words of affirmation, telling him he was so great and so smart and giving him a lot of encouragement.

"Sounds like you have a cold," she said in a concerned voice over the phone.

"Yeah," he said, his voice probably a little hoarse.

"Well, where's Joni?" she asked.

"She's at the studio taping."

"Well, if I was there," she said, "I would get you some hot lemon tea and honey."

Instead of replying with something like, "Oh, my sweetheart takes good care of me," Marcus said, "Oh, you would?" All of this sounds innocent enough, but that was the crack. That was when the enemy started planting seeds of doubt: "Does Joni really love me? Maybe she doesn't. Why wasn't she here for me?"

I can see how the two of them were ensnared by the enemy's lies. I know I'm not perfect, but I was healthy enough to know the affair wasn't about me. Marcus should have shared his need with me, and I would have dropped what I was doing and come to his side. Their emotional connection, me being away, Marcus being sick, and the door of opportunity being opened created the perfect storm.

When everything came out, to Marcus' tremendous credit, he did the right thing. He repented to God and to me, and he humbly submitted to godly counsel. He took responsibility for his sin. That was huge in our recovery. Another important step in rebuilding our relationship was that we became intentional about making time for each other, even though we were incredibly busy. Saturday turned into our weekly date day, when we made sure we put each other first—ahead of work, kids, and even ministry. Our number one ministry was now to each other. The number one place the Lord wants to love through us and grow us is in our relationships with those closest to us, particularly our spouses. That's ultimately what marriage is all about.

Next to God, I made sure I woke up to the need to put Marcus first. I never retaliated against the woman involved in any way. I've forgiven her, and Marcus took full responsibility for his actions. She moved away and has since found forgiveness and healing. I wish her only the best. We all made it through the storm with a few tattered sails along the way. Let me be clear, Marcus humbled himself through this process, and our love became stronger. We fought our way back, and after this horrific storm we helped many marriages. It took years to rebuild trust, and we definitely had scars, but God was faithful. We were married almost forty years when Marcus graduated to heaven.

STEPS THROUGH THE STORM

> The LORD your God, who goes before you, He will fight for you, according to all He did for you in Egypt before your eyes.
>
> —DEUTERONOMY 1:30

Yes, you have to shake off the enemy's snakes that latch on to your life. There are some things and people you have to just let go of and get on with life. However, there are other things and people that are most definitely worth fighting for. The Lord will let you know. Your natural mind and flesh may say, "Just quit. It hurts too much. Give up on them," but the Lord says, "They're worth fighting for." I'm sure glad the Lord didn't give up on me, that He felt I was worth fighting for! You were worth fighting for too. The Lord fought for you to the point that He sweat drops of blood in the Garden of Gethsemane and then went to the cross, where He defeated death and won the victory for you and me. We were worth fighting for, and the even better news is that the Lord goes before us and fights for us.

> *Lord, thank You for fighting for me when You died on the cross—and thank You for continuing to fight for me. As You guide me through the storms, show me what to fight for and what to shake off. Holy Spirit, I know You are helping me in my weakness and are praying for me as only You can. Amen.*

Chapter 8

GOING PUBLIC

HAVE YOU EVER been in a storm where the sky is dark, it's pouring rain, and right in the middle of it all the sun peeks out of the clouds and shoots down rays of light and hope? There's nothing more beautiful than sunlight piercing through a storm. That was Marcus and I during the three years we spent healing and growing our relationship. Walking through these emotions was brutal at times, but then it was beautiful. In the beginning there was not much sun peeking through. Eventually, though, there was more and more sunshine and less and less rain, until there was just a sprinkle and then nothing at all. At times we felt like newlyweds on our honeymoon.

Watching Marcus take responsibility for his failure and seeing the way he worked to regain my trust made me love him more than ever. We both loved each other more than ever. Because so much healing had taken place, we decided not to go public. Why should we? Marcus had repented and turned from his sin. Our counselors, ministry leaders, and other supportive people in our lives knew. We weren't being secretive, just protective. Now that we were finally on the other side of the storm, there was no need to broadcast our personal struggle to the world. That was our plan, anyway. Little did we know, new storm clouds were brewing. Things were about to get turbulent again. As we were to soon discover, both Marcus and Daystar were about to be involved in four lawsuits: three filed by three women who had been employed at Daystar and another filed by us to protect Daystar's interest.

As indicated in the papers filed in one of the lawsuits, one bright and promising day in 2010 our plans were abruptly interrupted by another unexpected phone call. This one was not from my parents but from our attorney. "Hey, I need you and Marcus to come to my office ASAP," he urged. "There's something important going on you guys need to know about." Neither of us had any idea what was going on.

When we got to his office, our attorney's face was ashen. "Y'all need to sit down," he said soberly, motioning to the chairs. "Look, I'm just going to get straight to the point. Another attorney came to see me, informing me that he's representing three women who know about Marcus' affair. They say they're going to file lawsuits and go public with this information unless we pay them millions of dollars."

It felt as if the air had been sucked out of the room. Then something rose up in me. "Hell can freeze over before we pay them a single penny!" I said. "I don't care if we have to deal with lawsuits and depositions forever." Marcus was silent, taking it all in. My immediate thought was, "This is pure blackmail," and I couldn't believe any attorney would actually present such a claim.

Fortunately we had experience with these kinds of attacks on the ministry. We had been through other lawsuits and, as I've mentioned, had never lost a single one, because we were clean in our business dealings and had followed the Lord's leading. This case was different, however, because it was personal. At that time, our struggle was only known to a few professional counselors who were involved in our marital healing process. As the filings in one of the lawsuits reveal, we saw it as a scheme these three women had created in an attempt to benefit financially from our pain and personal ordeal. As reflected in one of the pleadings, none of them had any involvement whatsoever in the affair itself or what Marcus and I went through because of it.

All three of these women had worked for us. And as indicated in pleadings, we were convinced they were all disgruntled over events that occurred before or in connection with their departure from employment at Daystar. Marcus and I firmly believed it would not be right for either us or Daystar to pay any money to keep this from going public. We believed we were right and relied on our pit bull attorney to protect our interests and flip the script on them. He was tough, savvy, and amazing. Plus, he probably knew more of the Bible than I did. More than anything, we had the Lord in our corner and trusted Him to take us through the drawn-out process of sending depositions back and forth, back and forth.

By that point, I knew it was time for us to tell our story. I knew it was the right thing to do. I wanted everything to be out in the open because if not, we'd always be looking over our shoulders. I preferred to just put it all out there and let the chips fall where they may because Marcus had done the right thing. After seeking the Lord, Marcus also felt going public was the right thing to do. We both would rather face the storm over making our private marital matters public than pay a dime.

We didn't have to go public, but we did. We went on *Good Morning America* with Robin Roberts, then *Dr. Phil* and other shows, including ours on Daystar.

Ultimately the lawsuits were ended with none of the women receiving any money or any monetary equivalent. But the process of going public about our personal marital issues was excruciating for Marcus because of all the shame. Though we were healed as a couple, going public about the indiscretion was like pulling the scab off an old wound. It was fitting that over a decade later the last message Marcus would preach was titled "How to Break the Shame Barrier."

Because he had struggled with shame and made it through that storm, Marcus was willing to talk about the situation initially, but he didn't want to keep talking about it. In other words, we weren't going to be the ministry that saved marriages. Yes, we would be used in that way, but that wouldn't be our focus. He wanted to keep the main thing the main thing. Marcus was an evangelist at heart, and his passion was to spread the gospel through television. That was his lane, and he knew it. Although it was crushing for him to be seen by the world in his failure and humble himself, he did it.

HEALING AND HOPE

When the lawsuits were filed against us, they named the woman Marcus had been involved with. Our attorney called and informed her, "Hey, we didn't say your name, but they have named you, so it's going to come out." She hadn't told her kids, and her new husband didn't know anything about it. I told our attorney to tell her I was sorry she would have to go through this three years after the incident. Our attorney told me she broke down and cried. I didn't have any animosity toward her. You realize you have truly forgiven when you don't want to see the person who hurt you hurt.

This was one of the greatest storms Marcus and I went through in our lives. When I look back and remember Marcus, I think of David. David was a man after God's own heart, yet he failed miserably. Instead of wallowing in despair, he brought his sin to the Lord and repented, which involved taking action to deal with his issues moving forward. As a result, God restored David and used him until the end of his days. I love Acts 13:36, which says, "For David, after he had served his own generation by the will of God, fell asleep, [and] was buried with his fathers." David, the one who messed up royally, still fulfilled God's will in his life.

This was Marcus. He messed up. It would cost him. But he did the right thing. He repented and took action toward correction, and God brought him back. That's why I'm writing about this. The Holy Spirit–inspired Scriptures didn't leave out David's flaws or the flaws of the other people God used. The truth is, almost every person God used was majorly flawed. Consider this:

- Abraham lied and threw his wife under the bus in order to protect his own skin (Gen. 20).

- Moses killed an Egyptian and fled (Exod. 2:11–22).

- David had an affair and set up the woman's husband to be killed in battle to cover up his sin (2 Sam. 11).

- Rahab was a prostitute (Josh. 2).

- Paul was a murderer (Acts 9).

- Peter denied Jesus three times (Luke 22:54–62).

I could go on.

Marcus also submitted to the accountability of the Church of God denomination, where he had ministry credentials. He called every major leader he could think of and told them what was going on, what had happened three years earlier, and that we'd gone through counseling and healing. Instead of condemning us, they wrapped their arms around us, and Marcus felt supported by so many. Still, the Church of God's recovery protocol required ministers going through this kind of situation to sit down for a certain amount of time.

Marcus could have gotten away with not submitting, but he did, and they were very gracious to him. Actually, he and I flew to Cleveland, Tennessee, and met with the board and leadership. They couldn't have been any kinder about our situation, and Marcus was completely restored. Even so, Marcus had to deal with such shame for so many years.

My point in writing this is to show that Marcus and I both understand the storm of personal betrayal, and you can get through it too. Think about it, Jesus was betrayed by His own disciples. He went through legal betrayal and was lied about, flogged and beaten, and then eventually crucified. Jesus went through public betrayal, humiliation, and death. Yet the Father resurrected and restored Him. From this we draw our strength. "Since he himself has gone through suffering and testing, he is able to help us when we are being tested" (Heb. 2:18, NLT). That suffering includes the suffering of personal betrayal.

Many people think that if you are transparent about a mistake you've made and confess your weakness publicly, people will judge and discredit you. That's what the enemy wants you to believe. But in reality, it's just the opposite. If you are authentic and truly repentant and share from a heart that is healed, it actually helps others heal and gives them hope.

For Marcus, this season was really hard because he was so ashamed of what he had done. Breaking the news to our kids was probably the most difficult thing he had to do. It broke his heart. Yet in reality they got to see their dad, whom they loved, as a human being who made a mistake but then did the right thing in the face of it. Our kids learned a great lesson. Number one: Dad wasn't perfect. Nobody is perfect, "for all have sinned and fall short of the glory of God" (Rom. 3:23). Again, all means all. It doesn't excuse his sin, but Marcus took ownership of it. Number two: when we make a mistake, we can be honest and real about it. The kids saw their father's repentance and a path they could follow that leads to restoration and healing.

The bottom line is that Marcus repented, submitted to counseling and leadership, and went through a restoration process. He and I were better on the other side of it. It wasn't a fun thing to go through, and I wouldn't want to go through it again, but it made us stronger and gave us a sensitivity to what others are going through that we otherwise would not have had.

Another strange thing I had to deal with personally when we decided to go public was all the people who treated me like poor little Joni whose husband is fooling around on her. I just thought, "OK, you all. It is what it is. God forgave him. I forgave him. He's dealt with it. Let's move on." Many people don't want to let you move on. While it was hard for me to watch Marcus suffer again, there is a price to pay for sin. I mean, you don't want people to go through that, but it should make you pause to think about the decisions you make, what will happen down the road as a result, and who will be affected. It's the ripple effect people don't always consider.

As a public person, even when you do the right thing, ask for forgiveness, and are restored, you still have to deal with criticism and judgment. It comes with the territory. So you have to develop a tough skin and decide to turn the situation around on the enemy and use it for good, being transparent and letting people know, "Hey, we survived. It wasn't easy, but God has restored us." That is the message that eventually came out of the affair. Years later people realized, "Yeah, they're good. You can tell they love each other." And we were better than before. I was better, and Marcus was better.

I think about how much Daystar grew from 2007 to 2021, when Marcus passed. I think about how if I had given up on the marriage or divorced him, it would have splintered our family and the ministry. The Lord told me, "He's worth fighting for." He was—we were—but we had to work through a process that included going public. The Lord used the storm of those lawsuits to push us out and make our story public.

STEPS THROUGH THE STORM

> For You, Lord, are good, and ready to forgive, and
> abundant in mercy to all those who call upon You.
> —PSALM 86:5

The storm of failure is one that smashes many on the
rocks and shipwrecks their faith. The enemy constantly
accuses us, saying, "You've blown it too badly this time.
Just look at yourself, you loser. You failed again. God
could never forgive you." Thank goodness our God's
magnanimous grace is bigger than man's. Nineteenth-
century preacher Charles Spurgeon said, "The rain of
His grace is always dropping; the river of His bounty is
ever-flowing, and the well-spring of His love is constantly
overflowing."[1] The Lord is always waiting for us with open
arms. He is "good, and ready to forgive, and abundant in
mercy to all those who call upon [Him]" (Ps. 86:5).

Failure can actually be a good thing if we fall to the
foot of the cross. When we exhibit genuine repentance
and humility, God will make us stronger and more effective. It's possible to love God dearly and still fail miserably. That was Peter's story. After he denied the Lord
three times, Peter "wept bitterly" (Luke 22:62). Yet days
after Jesus was risen, we see that same Peter saying to
Him, "Lord, You know all things; You know that I love
You," to which Jesus replied, "Feed My sheep" (John
21:17). Grace forgives and then gives an assignment.

> *Lord, You know that I love You, yet You*
> *remember that I am but dust. I thank You*
> *that when I fail and turn to You in repentance,*
> *instead of condemning me You are abundant*

89

in mercy and ready to forgive, not only to free me but also to use me. Amen.

Chapter 9

NO FEAR AND
SWIRLING ANGELS

CRIED NEARLY EVERY night for six months. I cried so many
tears that fluid began to fill my left eye, and it wouldn't
drain. I was trying to host a TV show with this puffy red
puddle on my face, and it just looked horrible. Because my eye
refused to heal, I went to the eye doctor, and he had to lance it
with a needle to drain it. I asked him why this was happening—
Was it because I was crying so often? He said that was probably why.

After about seven months I finally started getting better, and
that's when the Lord began leading me to take some serious
new steps forward in my life. But before we get to that, I need
to take you back to how it all started and explain why there
were so many tears.

Despite everything Marcus and I had gone through, we were
healed, and Daystar experienced another growth spurt. Instead
of being destroyed as the enemy had desired, we became that
cracked vessel with light shining through, and people related
to our realness. We weren't some pie-in-the-sky super saints;
we were people just like them. All over the world souls were
being saved, miraculous signs were occurring, and people were

being ministered to like never before. The favor of God was on Daystar, and the Holy Spirit was drawing people to Himself.

Each of our three children—Jonathan, Rachel, and Rebecca—felt called to come beside us in this ministry, and they did. Then we watched all of them marry wonderful people and have incredible children. My grandchildren are amazing, you know. They're the prettiest and smartest kids on the planet! Marcus and I were now grandparents doing the empty nester thing and enjoying every moment of it. We loved being with each other.

In March of 2020, Marcus and I were in South Africa ministering at several of the country's largest churches. I was speaking at women's conferences, and Marcus was preaching on Sundays. The Holy Spirit was moving, and it was a powerful time; however, it would be the last thing we did together overseas.

One day our kids called and said, "Y'all better get back here fast! Things are closing down."

So we said, "We're coming. We're coming."

Marcus had a golf game scheduled, and I told him, "We need to go. You don't need to play golf."

"We'll be fine," he said.

"No, Marcus. We have to go."

But he didn't relent. He played golf on our final day in South Africa, and we flew home the next morning. When we arrived at the Dallas-Fort Worth airport, we couldn't believe what met us. The place was basically empty, appearing eerily abandoned. We returned to the United States one day before it closed because of COVID-19. If we had not left South Africa when we did, we wouldn't have been able to get back into the United

States for a long time. The world we knew was about to change in a way we couldn't have imagined. I don't think any of us really expected the whole world to shut down as it did.

The world was indeed changing. People's lives would be drastically altered. Businesses were forced to close; stadiums were empty; churches were ordered to stop gathering. It was crazy. Politicians were calling it the "new normal." Yet just as the Lord had guided Marcus to that little diamond-in-the-rough station in Decatur, Texas, the world's "new normal" would prove to be a new opportunity for Daystar. We were marooned on our island of Malta, and just as it was with the apostle Paul, souls were waiting, and a door for ministry swung wide open for us.

Because Daystar was a television station, the FCC required us to stay open. No problem! Our staff was able to keep coming in to work, and we were able to keep broadcasting. Meanwhile, people were locked in their homes, watching more television than ever before, and that included Daystar. Many people were fearful and worried about the future. We immediately picked up on their desperate need for hope.

"Let's minister where people are," Marcus told me. "People are stuck at home, so they're watching more television, looking for answers. Let's give them the answer." It was at that point we changed the name of our show from *Marcus and Joni* to *Ministry Now*. After that, things really began to expand, and we held on for the ride. Marcus was right. We were providing something fearful hearts were searching for. During that time, at three o'clock one morning the Lord downloaded to me the song "No Fear." Here's a portion of the lyrics:

You have given us Your power

THROUGH THE STORM

Your glory, a sound mind
Your supernatural love
You will never ever leave us
Forsake us, forget us
We're covered by Your blood

In the middle of the battle
When the fight is on
When the burden's heavy
I am not alone
In the middle of the battle
When the fight is on
When the burden's heavy
I will sing this song

No weapon formed against will prosper
We are victorious in You

You have given us Your power
Your glory, a sound mind
Your supernatural love
You will never ever leave us
Forsake us, forget us
We're covered by Your blood...

No fear
I know that You are with me
No fear
You've given me Your Spirit
No fear
Your love has overtaken
And I will not be shaken
No fear[1]

Of course the song comes from the scripture "For God has not given us a spirit of fear, but of power and of love and of a sound mind" (2 Tim. 1:7). I didn't know it at the time, but I was probably writing that song as much for myself as I was for the world. Thousands have been blessed by that song. You can never go wrong singing a song that's based in Scripture. Daystar was broadcasting a message of hope, and hope was a person. There was no need to fear, because that person is Jesus, and He promised to carry all of us through the storm. His presence would show up right in our homes. We weren't alone. That was our message.

AN UNEXPECTED MINISTRY OPPORTUNITY

Right in the midst of offering hope, which has always been the foundation of what we do, we saw another much-needed door of ministry swing open. So much confusing, misleading, and just plain false information regarding COVID-19 was bombarding the world. All of us watched in horror as that terrible virus was politicized to push agendas and weaponized to control us. *Ministry Now* became a place for viewers seeking an alternative, truthful voice outside the biased mainstream media. I don't want to spend too much time on this, but I need to touch on it because it's important to this story.

The fact that we were willing to share truths that were being censored during that time gave us a huge audience. People were desperate for actual answers, and Daystar was one of the few places they could go and hear what doctors were really saying and what alternative treatments were available. For example, all over the world ivermectin and hydroxychloroquine had already been used effectively against the virus. The documented reports didn't lie, but these types of treatments went against Big Pharma and big government's agenda to control.

When the COVID-19 vaccine came around, I knew from the interviews I had already done that most holistic and naturopathic doctors and even many traditional medical doctors cautioned against taking it. The mRNA technology it uses is very controversial, and some believe it can infect our God-given immune systems with long-term problems. I believed it was really a weapon. We started having doctors on the show who had no agenda other than to save lives the most natural and effective way possible.

Dr. Simone Gold from California was one. Dr. Richard Bartlett, who talked about using budesonide, was another. Dr. Pierre Kory was one who said ivermectin would be a life-saver as an early protocol. He found that it helped people, even saved lives. But then the mainstream news started dogging all of these alternative treatments. Politician Robert Kennedy Jr. knows about this very well. We were saying one thing, and the world was saying something totally different.

Masks were a joke. You can't protect anybody from COVID with a mask. Even if you walk in a restaurant with one on, when you sit down, you take it off. But somehow the virus magically isn't down there where you're sitting; it's up there where you're standing while you wait for your table. People were driving alone in their cars with masks on. The public was being led by fear, fear, fear instead of following the science and common sense.

We ministered and allowed information to be presented that was not being discussed in the secular media. Dr. Peter

McCullough, a highly respected cardiologist in Dallas, was vilified horribly for following the science. I interviewed British scientist Michael Yeadon, a former vice president of Pfizer in the UK, who said of the mRNA vaccines, "I believe they're irredeemably dangerous, bluntly."[2] I could name doctor after doctor who took a chance on losing everything, including their licenses, for telling the truth.

Of course, we were labeled as conspiracy theorists. All the while, however, a steady stream of people were telling us, "You saved our lives. We wouldn't have known if you hadn't given us that information." Staying on the course we felt the Lord had laid out for us led us into a storm, but I never veered or backed down. Marcus always supported me in this because he knew how passionate I was about trying to help people. We did that through 2021. Now, thankfully, the truth is starting to come out, and we are being validated by undeniable data. It seems much of the public is finally waking up and changing their tune.

I was the one who got COVID first. And of course, because I'd had so many brilliant doctors and scientists on the show, I immediately used some of the protocols we knew about. Ivermectin was administered early, along with a steady dose of vitamins C and D. Fortunately, it was like a mild case of the flu and lasted only for about a week without causing any breathing issues.

Marcus and I did the whole quarantine and keep-your-distance deal like we were supposed to, but he eventually got sick too. However, he kept testing negative, negative, negative. Finally he tested positive, and we started treating him with the same protocol I was on. He seemed to be doing well, but Marcus had type 2 diabetes. That was not good, particularly with the delta strain of COVID, which was the worst.

But there's another important factor that most people don't know. About a year earlier, Marcus had a bad case of hiccups. It was nonstop for a whole day—twenty-four hours. We thought it was the weirdest thing, but because the hiccups went away after a day, we didn't take it too seriously. Then, right before he got COVID, Marcus had the hiccups again, this time for a good forty-eight hours straight. It was horrible. I felt so bad hearing him hiccup, especially during the night. I was praying for him. We even mentioned it on the program, asking people to pray for him because the hiccups would not stop. We later discovered that when this happens, the vagus nerve is trying to tell you there's something going on with the heart. It's a rare condition. So there was something going on with Marcus' heart that we did not know about before he got COVID.

We were treating Marcus, and he seemed to be getting better. He even appeared to be coming out of it, but then we noticed his breathing becoming a little more labored. When his oxygen dropped to 82, I called his doctors. They told us we needed to go to the ER immediately because he needed to be on oxygen. When the ambulance arrived, the paramedics hooked him up to oxygen and let me ride to the hospital with him. The whole way, Marcus was talking and coherent.

By the time we got to the ER, Marcus' oxygen was up in the 90s. They admitted him anyway, and he wanted me to go to the room with him.

"You know you can't go up," the nurse said, a little abrupt and bossy. "It's our procedure."

"OK," I said, but I was thinking, "That's a terrible procedure."

The nurses took Marcus away, and I went back to the house, thinking he would only be in the hospital for a short time; I'd probably pick him up the next day.

An hour or so later, Rachel called me and said she had called the hospital, asking about her dad and got to talking to one of the nurses. "We can allow your mom to come," the nurse said, "but if she comes in, she can't go out."

"Get your suitcase, Mom," Rachel said. "I'll come pick you up and take you to the hospital. You can be with Dad." It was the Lord's favor. I jumped up and packed a few things to spend the night at the hospital, and Rachel arrived within five minutes. We went straight to the hospital, she dropped me off, and I went up to his room. Again, I figured I would be there only a short time, maybe one night or two at the most.

It was the craziest thing. When I walked in, they had a mask on Marcus on top of the oxygen, and he was tied down with restraints that looked like handcuffs. I couldn't believe it. I was told this was done because Marcus kept trying to get up. They had also given him a sedative, so he was knocked out. Marcus rarely took any kind of medication, so even the slightest dose would pack a punch. I took the restraints off and sat by his bed, but he wasn't aware. Throughout the night the rhythmic sound of the oxygen pump kept me company as I watched Marcus. It was clear he was struggling.

The next day he started coming out of the sedation a little bit but was still largely incoherent. By the third day, however, he was sitting up and talking. The nurses and I informed him of what was going on, and of course he immediately wanted to go home. But we said, "No, we have to wait on your oxygen to get better." Over the next few days, he was coherent. He was able to eat, but his breathing was still labored, and his oxygen level continued to vacillate.

Rachel gathered friends to pray in the hospital parking lot, and I would look out Marcus' hospital window and wave at them. No visitors were allowed in his room until he tested negative for COVID. But Rachel was at the hospital every day, either outside in the parking lot or in his room when she was later allowed in. Jonathan also came to see his dad, and Rebecca did as well, even though he was on the COVID wing and she was pregnant. All the kids were praying. The whole world was praying.

As the days crept by, Marcus seemed to be getting better. He hated the oxygen tube being on him and was always pulling at it. When the doctors x-rayed his lungs, they were now clear, and he tested negative for COVID. The doctors were hoping to start decreasing the oxygen, but strangely Marcus' breathing was still an issue.

Now that Marcus was COVID-free, there was a steady stream of our children coming up to pray for him. Then one night around Thanksgiving, Marcus' oxygen dropped way down. Troy Brewer sent some men up to the room, and Robert Morris came to pray for Marcus. All the family was there as well. When we gathered around him and started praying, his oxygen was just over 50 percent; then as we called out to God, it shot up to around 99 percent! It was an incredible moment. The Lord's presence was tangible. Even the nurses felt the peace in the room. But Marcus still needed to receive high levels of oxygen because if the doctors removed it, his oxygen level would drop again.

At this point the kids would come and switch out. Rachel's husband, Josh, and Jonathan's wife, Suzy, would stay with me at night so I could get some sleep. During this time, Marcus told us he saw angels swirling around him. He actually got Rachel to send texts out to people saying he saw angels swirling around him and at the top of the ceiling. "I thought I could die," he told us, "and the angels brought me comfort." One night I was lying on the hospital cot, trying to get some sleep when a bright light suddenly came into the room that made me open my eyes. There was definitely a presence there. It was probably an angel.

Marcus kept asking to go home. He'd say, "Do you know where my clothes are? Have you got the car here?"

"Yes, sweetheart," I would answer.

"You've got my shoes?" he said. "I need you to take me home."

I said, "Well, honey, I can't take you home just yet."

Marcus fully intended to get out of the hospital. He had a definite directive. He told us, "I want to do even more for Israel. I want to focus on souls. We will never be ashamed of the Holy Spirit. I want to stand for revival." Those are all the things he was planning to do when he got out.

There's a little story. On the third day, I was at the hospital alone with Marcus. I was so tired and had just fallen asleep when I heard his machine go off. I looked up, and Marcus was getting out of the bed, putting his leg over the side with the oxygen on, so he could go use the bathroom. He fainted immediately when he stood up because he had no oxygen. I jumped up and ran just in time to catch him from behind and brought him slowly to the ground. He wasn't that big, just about 140 pounds, but I barely caught him. All the alarms were going off, and I opened the door and yelled, "Help!" It took three men to get him back in the bed because he was so out of it.

Another night, Suzy was staying with me, trying to let me get some sleep. She was sitting right beside Marcus' bed. Marcus would wake up every few hours and say, "Where's Joni? Joni? Where's Joni?"

"Honey, I'm right here sleeping," I said.

"Well, let me go over there with you."

"Honey, you wouldn't want to sleep on this bed," I said. It was the worst little cot you've ever seen, but I was thankful for it.

Marcus was such a brilliant person, but he would get so angry because we wouldn't take him home. He'd say, "I want to go home. I want to go home." He called Jonathan up there, thinking for sure he'd get him out of the hospital.

"I can't," Jonathan told him.

"You are my son, and you're not doing what I ask you to do!" Marcus said.

We had a lot of funny moments like that.

We were in the hospital room for seventeen days. On November 30, my son-in-law Josh was staying in the room with me. When Marcus' oxygen would drop low, we would stand up and pray in the Spirit around his bed. That's all we really knew to do. We also had worship music playing all the time. Peace came, and we were resting. At 4 a.m., Josh was sitting right beside Marcus and I was sleeping when all of a sudden the alarm went off. I jumped up, and within seconds the medical personnel came rushing into the room with all their life-saving paraphernalia. There were probably ten people in the room.

Marcus was unresponsive. I was standing, looking, watching. Josh was standing with me. We were just praying. One thing I can absolutely tell you is that there was no fear in the room—none. There was no panic, only the incredible peace the Bible talks about, the peace that passes all understanding. It doesn't make sense. In my mind I knew without a doubt that they were going to revive Marcus and he was going to come home. I was convinced he was going to be fine. I knew people were praying for him all over the world.

The medical team was desperately working on Marcus, trying to just get a pulse so they could use the defibrillator paddles. They shot adrenaline into him and did everything they could, but his heart just stopped. The cardiologists told me Marcus had a cardiac event. That is different from a heart attack. According to the American Heart Association: "A heart attack is when blood flow to the heart is blocked. Sudden cardiac arrest is when the heart malfunctions and suddenly stops beating....With its pumping action disrupted, the heart can't pump blood to the brain, lungs and other organs. When this occurs, a person loses consciousness and has no pulse. Death occurs within minutes if the victim doesn't receive treatment."[3]

Despite all the medical team's efforts, they couldn't bring Marcus' heart back. It was just gone. The adrenaline, the defibrillator paddles—nothing worked. Josh and I stood there praying in the Spirit for five minutes, ten minutes, twenty, thirty. After forty-five minutes we knew Marcus was gone; he had graduated to heaven.

"TRUST ME, JONI"

The news shot out to the world that Marcus died from COVID. He did not. He was hospitalized for COVID, was recovering, and died of heart failure. He was well over the virus, and his lungs had been clear. He'd gotten the best treatment; we made sure of that. His heart just died from a preexisting condition that the virus contributed to.

I had interviewed many people over the previous thirty years who'd had near-death experiences who talked about how a person's spirit leaves his body. When I looked at Marcus' body, I knew he wasn't there. He was gone. I was in shock—really in shock. After forty-five minutes of trying to resuscitate him, the medical team looked at me, and I said, "If you guys could just leave the room, I would appreciate you letting us have some time." They were gracious.

By that time, Rachel had gotten there; then Jonathan arrived, then Suzy, and finally Rebecca. That was the hardest part, the kids coming in, because they didn't have any idea. The whole world was praying for Marcus. None of us thought there was any way it was his time to go. Rebecca and Suzy just wailed. Rachel was crying and inconsolable, and I was numb with shock. Rebecca eventually went over to the bed and lay over her dad. It was heartbreaking to watch.

A lot of people question God or get angry at Him after a loved one passes away. I can honestly say I was never angry. I hurt. There was pain. I had questions for God, as Job did, but I never questioned Him or His character. There is a difference. In the midst of all the emotions and grief I heard His still, small, comforting voice saying, "Trust Me, Joni. Trust Me."

"Yes, Lord," I said through tears. "But my sweetheart is gone."

The truth is, this life is a puff, a vapor, as James wrote (Jas. 4:14). Life is really about eternity. I never felt the truth of that statement any more than when I left that hospital room. As I walked out, my heart was ripping in two, but at the same time I was saying, "OK, Lord. He's gone." It wasn't that I was being cold. I was simply numb, and the Holy Spirit was helping me keep it together. I would fall apart later.

Everything after that seemed like a blur. I remember a wave of people calling and texting. I mean, the whole world had been praying for Marcus. It was just so humbling, really, to see the outpouring of love and support.

Jonathan and Suzy were supposed to host the show that morning because I obviously wasn't there to host. "Well, I guess we're not going to do a show," Jonathan told me.

"No, we need to tell the world what's going on," I said. "We need to let them know what happened, because everyone is going to give their narrative, and we need to tell what happened."

"Well, then, Mom, you need to come," he said.

It was almost as though I had heard Marcus say, "Yes, sweetheart, you need to do this." So I went. I didn't think about it or contemplate how hard it was going to be, whether I would fall apart before the world. I just said, "OK, I'll be there at the top of the show to tell everyone what happened."

I knew I wanted to represent Marcus and the Lord in a way that would be pleasing to Him. I went to the studio and walked right past everyone—even my friends—straight to the set. I couldn't look at anybody. It was as if the Lord had said, "Just stay focused. Go straight to the platform." Because I'm so relational, I knew that if I stopped to look or talk, I would break down. So I just had to get on the air and tell what had happened. Jonathan was with me, and we shared with the world that Marcus had finished his race and was with the Lord. And then I left while Jonathan and Suzy went on and hosted the show.

When I stepped off the set, my friends were all there waiting for me. And then, of course, I fell apart, and they grieved with me. Then I went home.

Driving up to the house felt surreal. It was Christmastime, and the decorations were up. I'm usually over-the-top about Christmas, but as I pulled into the driveway, I was thinking, "Wow, Marcus is not going to be here for Christmas. I don't want to see these right now. Please go away." But of course the decorations stayed, and I went into the empty house.

STEPS THROUGH THE STORM

> Be strong and of good courage, do not fear nor be afraid of them; for the LORD your God, He is the One who goes with you. He will not leave you nor forsake you.
>
> —DEUTERONOMY 31:6

God gives grace for real crises, not imaginary ones. Many of our storms are created in our own minds, causing untold anxiety, and they never actually materialize. Mark Twain once said, "I've lived through some terrible things in my life, some of which actually happened."[4] We laugh, but it's true. One thing is for certain, though: when a real storm materializes, God will show up in the storm with you. He will never leave you or forsake you. He showed up for me in the hospital room with Marcus and was with me after he passed. And He showed up for Marcus with comforting angels to escort him home. In both life and death, the Lord will be with you.

Lord, we know our days are numbered by You. We don't have to live in fear of death because our lives are secure in You for eternity. Lord, comfort those who have lost someone unexpectedly. Embrace them with Your peace that passes understanding and send ministering angels to stand by their side. Amen.

Chapter 10

FINISHING WELL

THE HOUSE WAS deathly quiet. I guess I didn't realize how big Marcus' personality was in our home. I think we tend to take those things for granted. He was enthusiastic and full of vision and always had something going on. His presence filled the atmosphere, and there was laughter—a lot of laughter.

Marcus died in November of 2021, and our forty-year anniversary would have been the following August. We were married for over thirty-nine years and had dated for two years before that. I'd spent forty-one years with this person, and then, without warning, he was gone. It left an instant crater in my soul. I didn't get any real sleep during the seventeen days we spent in the hospital, and it was all starting to catch up with me, so I just crashed in the bed. Over the next several days family and friends came by, bringing food and offering emotional support, but that first night I was home alone, and that's what I wanted. I wanted to be alone.

Outside our home is a beautiful garden patio that faces the swimming pool. It was our backyard retreat. Marcus and I would sit out there in the mornings and sip our coffee. We would also play cornhole together out there in the afternoons.

That's where you toss little beanbags into a hole on an inclined board. If you have good aim, the beanbag hits the board and slides into the hole. It's basically a safer version of horseshoes. We loved it. While playing, we would catch up on everything—which guests we'd have on the show, the latest news, and so on. It was our place to just unwind a bit.

After the deaths of my dad, my brother, and our friend John Paul Jackson, red birds became unusually significant to me. The Lord used them to confirm something very personal. There was one particular red bird that kept returning to our patio. Marcus and I would be out on the patio drinking coffee or playing cornhole, and my red bird would show up. We would kid about it, and I'd say, "Oh, there's my red bird. It's a sign from heaven." Each time I saw it, I would reflect on those I loved who had gone before us.

Marcus would say, "There's your red bird. You're going to win." And then he'd say, "I want a bird too. I want my own bird."

One day while we were out on the patio, a little black-and-white bird with a loud and quite particular chirp showed up. When Marcus saw it, he said, "That's my bird!"

I said, "OK, you can have that bird." We both laughed. So, I had the red bird, and Marcus had the chirpy bird, which I later discovered was a black-and-white whip-poor-will.

The morning after my first night without Marcus, I fixed my coffee and walked out on the patio. As I shuffled from the kitchen toward the patio, I said to myself, "I don't know if I want to go out there." At that moment, I felt the Holy Spirit speak gently: "Go out there. I have something for you."

I thought, "OK, Lord," and kept walking.

While sipping my coffee on the patio, I heard Marcus' bird. It was the whip-poor-will. I had my phone and decided to record a video of Marcus' bird. Just as I began to record, my red bird flew over and sat right next to Marcus' bird on the bush. Whip-poor-wills and red birds typically avoid each other. It was as if the Lord was giving me a little wink, a God wink, on the day after Marcus' death. It comforted my heart in the midst of the vacuum left by Marcus' absence. I felt the Lord say, "I've got you, Joni." And I felt His presence.

As I mentioned, friends and family came over to visit in the days that followed. It was a steady stream of refreshing love: Jonathan and Suzy, Rebecca and Jonathan, Rachel and Josh, my mom, close friends, my sister, and Marcus' brother, Gary. We all just came together and leaned on each other. I'm so thankful for my family and friends.

I made the decision early on to continue going in to Daystar each day to host *Ministry Now* and *Table Talk*. People would ask, "How can you do that?" Some said I should have gone on a sabbatical. But if I had gone on sabbatical, I would have gone into depression. I needed to do what I'm called to do. God shows up even more powerfully when we're in the midst of the storm. His presence is so close. He's right there beside you. And if you'll close your eyes and be still, you will hear Him whisper in your ear and know what to do. So I began to minister to others out of my pain, out of my grief—and now with deeper empathy and greater insight.

Paul wrote, "Blessed be the God and Father of our Lord Jesus Christ, the Father of mercies and God of all comfort, who comforts us in all our tribulation, that we may be able to comfort those who are in any trouble, with the comfort with which we ourselves are comforted by God" (2 Cor. 1:3–4). That's what I tried to do as I found comfort in the Lord. The Father comforts us in our pain, and He does it through the Holy Spirit, the Comforter, inside us. (See John 14:26.) Because He's inside us, the Holy Spirit comforts us while we walk in relationship with Him. (See Galatians 5:25.) Then we become conduits of comfort to others. Our greatest healing comes when we shift from having an inward focus on ourselves to an outward focus on others.

Letting the Lord do that healing work and moving forward with the life He has for you doesn't diminish your grief or pain. I continued doing what I was called to do, but don't believe for a moment that I wasn't grieving. At the risk of sounding redundant, I cried for six months straight, to the point that fluid built up around my eye and wouldn't drain.

I know from personal experience that God shows up in our most painful moments. As I said, if I had gone on a sabbatical with nothing specific to do, I would have become self-absorbed. Giving and blessing others helped heal my heart. Actually, the hardest part was going home at night after the show. At the studio there were people. I was doing interviews, singing worship songs, and working on production. I was busy. Then I would go home to the emptiness of the house, and all the emotions would jump on me. Going home was most definitely the hardest thing. I grieved, but not as one without hope. (See 1 Thessalonians 4:13–18.)

Marcus died November 30, 2021, and we held his funeral ten days later, on December 10. Pulling off a funeral of that magnitude in a short amount of time took a miracle. I knew I could fall apart later, but not that week. Again, the Lord carried me through. My prayer became something like, "Lord, I need You to do this today. Unless You do it, it won't get done, because this is way bigger than me. That seems to be the story of my life. Yet I trust what Your Word says, that I'm 'kept by the Holy Spirit who dwells in [me]' [2 Tim. 1:14]. Holy Spirit, You are keeping me, guiding me, and empowering me today. In my weakness and grief I choose to press forward diligently with full confidence in You. Amen."

Of course, many wonderful people stepped up to help, including my producer, Rose. Really, she and I planned the whole service. I had to be centrally involved because I knew Marcus the best and wanted this funeral to honor him in the way he deserved.

Somehow the details all came together, and I found myself sitting in Gateway Church along with thousands of others there to celebrate the life of Marcus Lamb. I've never seen so many ministers gathered together in one place to honor a great man, a man who loved God with all his heart. It was the most anointed funeral I have ever seen. While I was sitting in the service, I was thinking to myself, "Lord, I hope You will let Marcus peek over for just a moment so he can see how honored and loved he has been." It seemed every major minister was there: Joyce Meyer, Marilyn Hickey, David Jeremiah, John Hagee, Joel Osteen, Robert Morris, Jimmy Evans, Perry Stone— the list went on and on. There were rows and rows of ministers we had interviewed over the years. I was trying to take in every moment, but I was still a little in shock. The reality still hadn't sunk in.

Words can't describe how the presence of God fell in that place. You really need to go to YouTube and watch the service.

It has been viewed almost a million times, and thousands of people commented that they couldn't stop crying because of the powerful anointing of the Holy Spirit. From the beginning, when the legendary Phil Driscoll worshipped with his trumpet and sang "I Exalt Thee," the Holy Spirit just dropped down like a warm blanket.

Tears were flowing freely, but they were not tears of sadness but rather of hope, joy, and praise. We knew where Marcus was. Our hope wasn't wishful thinking; it was grounded in the reality and faithfulness of the Lord. Seeing what God had done for us in the past, we had an expectant hope while the storm was raging. "Wait and hope for and expect the Lord," the psalmist wrote, "be brave and of good *courage* and let your heart be stout and enduring. Yes, wait for and hope for and expect the Lord" (Ps. 27:14, AMPC, emphasis added)! Our hope is based on faith—not blind faith but on a sure reality and God's promises. As the writer of Hebrews proclaimed, "Now faith is the substance of things hoped for, the evidence of things not seen" (Heb. 11:1).

I remember one particular example of the Holy Spirit guiding me. It seemed like a little thing, but it ended up being huge. After Rose and I had developed the whole program, a friend called me and said, "Hey, Phil Driscoll wanted me to let you know he's going to be at the funeral if you want anything." I said, "Well, yes, we want him to do something." So Phil started the service, and the presence of God filled the place. I mean, it was amazing. The whole service was beautiful and honored a life well lived. Everything was totally set up by the Lord.

Pastor Robert Morris said the opening prayer, and his words were equally anointed. I keep using the word *anointed* because only the Holy Spirit could have orchestrated a service like that. Pastor Morris really defined who Marcus was, and I thought his words were fitting to share.

"There were some things about Marcus that I just have to mention," Pastor Robert said. "There was no way you could be around him and not pick up on these things. Number one, he loved Jesus. In personal conversations or on television, I cannot recall how many times he would get choked up and emotional talking about the Lord and what the Lord had done in his life and how grateful he was for the Lord....Secondly, you couldn't be around Marcus without picking up [on] how much he loved Joni. He went on just a little too much sometimes about Joni. He loved Joni. She was the love of his life on this earth, and she was his partner....Number three, he loved his sons and daughters. The reason I say sons, plural, and daughters is because the three of you became six, and he saw no difference in the ones that married in and the ones that were born in....He was always so proud of them....The fourth thing you couldn't be around Marcus and not pick up on is how much he loved Israel. He loved the Jewish people."[1]

The other speakers—including Jimmy Evans, Joel Osteen, his family members, and John Hagee—continued with the same worshipful anointing. Jentezen Franklin gave the eulogy. One of the things Jentezen explained was how in the beginning he and Marcus were just two country boys from the Church of God, excited about serving the Lord. Jentezen was a country preacher at a small church in a small Georgia town when Marcus called him to come preach on his station in Montgomery. The station was small, just like Jentezen's church, but they were both passionate about what God was doing. When Marcus told him we were moving to Dallas to start a station, Jentezen said, "If Marcus had not had Joni, I would have thought, 'He's gone off the deep end just like all those other preachers.' But I knew she was the anchor, and she knew that they had heard from God to go to Dallas, Texas. No station permit, nothing but a word from God...But boy, the anointing of God that was on them was so real and the vision was so powerful, here we stand today," with Daystar broadcasting all over the world![2]

After that, the Holy Spirit through Jason Crabb had us all in tears as he sang "I Bowed on My Knees and Cried Holy." In the end we had accomplished what we had set out to do. The Holy Spirit had guided us in honoring Marcus' life, just as He has guided us in everything else.

After the funeral I had to return to reality. People were looking at me, wondering how I was going to address everything. In that moment, I felt as if the Lord said, "All I want you to do, Joni, is just get up every morning. I'll get up with you. And then take it one step at a time."

We received thousands of encouraging cards and letters in those first weeks. Some really stood out. I remember one from a woman in Canada who said, "I was really upset when Marcus died." She went to the Lord and asked, "How could You let this happen?" She went into her prayer closet, and the Lord answered, "If I Am, then you have to know he's here rejoicing with Me. And nothing and no one could have plucked him out of My hand. And I have not left Daystar without a leader."

Reading that letter was so humbling and sobering. It still is. I received that as another nudge from the Lord that continuing forward was the right thing.

I finally came to the place where I understood that Marcus had finished his race. Based on the life he lived, what I saw through the years as we worked together building Daystar, the way he responded to challenges and hard times, and so many other things, there's no way I would ever believe the enemy had taken him out. Marcus was about to celebrate fifty years in ministry and forty years of marriage. He had run hard and fast for a long time, and he finished his race. We may not like God's timetable, but I know Marcus finished his course and that he finished well. I take comfort in that. People can say, "Oh, but he should have lived longer. He was only sixty-four." But he accomplished more in the sixty-four years he was on this earth than most people could in two or three lifetimes. Thinking about that helped me move on.

When the funeral was over, there were family and friends and food. But I was now in the full-blown grieving process. At home the presence of God was there with me, replacing my loneliness. But I still had to go through the grieving process.

I have a dear friend named Rhonda Davis whose husband, Hank, passed a month before Marcus. In fact, Marcus officiated at her husband's funeral. Hank's death was also surreal because he and Rhonda have been such good friends of ours for so many years. It was really a godsend to have someone to talk to who understood the grieving process because Rhonda was walking through it herself. I had other precious friends too, but because Rhonda had just lost Hank and, like me, had ministered alongside her husband and seen miracles happen, we could sit and cry on the phone together and talk about our feelings. Having her to talk with was very healing. She was, and is, a true friend who walked with me, and I with her.

During that time, the Lord prompted a prophetic minister named Hubie Synn to call me. Hubie has been used world-wide in the prophetic and has been on *Table Talk* a couple of times. Walking through an airport one night, Hubie saw a Jewish man sitting in black attire. The Holy Spirit prompted Hubie to tell the man he had an unpublished book that was going to change the world. Then the Lord began to give Hubie specific steps for the man to take regarding publishing and ministry. Hubie had no idea that the man had a manuscript in his briefcase and was crying out to God about what to do with it. That man was Jonathan Cahn, and the manuscript was *The Harbinger*, which did, in fact, impact the world.

Hubie said in part, "Basically, the Lord is going to have to put your heart back together because losing a spouse is different from any other loss; half your heart goes."[3] He shared much more from the Lord with me, but I'll talk about that later. It did feel as though half my heart was gone; I was one person instead of the couple we had been. Marcus and I were one, but now he was gone. My kids would say, "Well, Mom, if you're lonely, we can come over if you want." It was really wonderful to be with my children and grandchildren, but it wasn't the same. It's *not* the same. That half-a-heart thing is the hard thing to get over. Hubie said, "God's going to put it back together." He intimated that there would be something coming, but I didn't know what. God is so faithful. He showed up for me every day, and many times in the form of others.

There's a passage in Psalms that describes our journey as

God's children: "Blessed are those whose strength is in you, whose hearts are set on pilgrimage. As they pass through the Valley of Baka, they make it a place of springs; the autumn rains also cover it with pools. They go from strength to strength" (Ps. 84:5–7, NIV). When our hearts are set on pilgrimage—which means we take God's hand on this journey until the end, regardless of what we are going through—when we go through the Valley of Baca (translated "the valley of weeping"), God turns it into a place of springs and refreshment.

Bible teacher Warren Wiersbe wrote that the Valley of Baca "is a name for any difficult and painful place in life, where everything seems hopeless and you feel helpless."[4] That sounds like a storm to me. God wants to meet us there and turn those difficult valleys into places of refreshment for us and others. It's possible that the Valley of Baca wasn't an actual geographical location but a figurative place like the pit of despair. Losing Marcus was a valley of weeping for sure, but friends were a spring in my valley.

About seven months into my grieving process, my eye had healed. I went outside and lay in the driveway because the sun sets on the front side of our house. Marcus and I used to go out there sometimes at night and lie on the driveway. That evening I prayed, "God, what are You doing? Could You please tell Your girl what's going on? I'm not questioning You; I just need to understand." Softly and gently He spoke those same two words to my spirit: "Trust Me." Then He said, "I'm going to help you; just trust Me." I'd like to tell you He gave me some great theological truth, but that's what He said. He didn't tell me what He was planning to do, or when; He just said, "Trust Me." I never questioned the Lord's sovereignty or character because I had seen so many miracles throughout my life with Marcus. I knew God was in control of the situation.

All I can say is a supernatural grace has carried me since the day of the funeral. It was a grace that would continue to carry me forward one day at a time into the unknown. During the storm of Marcus' passing, I felt a huge responsibility to the platform God had given us and our family. Marcus had left clear instructions six months before his homegoing that in the event he left this earth before me, I was to lead Daystar. I never dreamed I would be in this position, but I trusted my husband, and I trusted God. It was his hope that one day when we were both gone, our children would continue the legacy of Daystar.

After his passing I knew a lot of people were watching. I was obedient to get up when I didn't feel like getting up. I was obedient to go on camera when my eyes were all messed up and still host those shows. I was just obedient to do what I knew was the next right thing to do, even though it wasn't necessarily fun or pleasant or what I felt like doing. I didn't lean on my emotions at that point; I followed what I knew was right. I didn't have a deep theological insight, only a word from God to take it one day at a time and trust Him.

Then the Lord told me, "I need you to get your house in order."

Surprised, I asked, "What do You mean? I thought my house was in order."

"No," the Holy Spirit pressed. "I need you to start taking better care of yourself."

At that I gave up sugar, white bread, white flour, and pasta and started eating more vegetables and fish, drinking more water, and exercising. I started doing that about seven months after Marcus passed and didn't really know why. All I knew was that the Lord had said, "I've got some things for you to do, and I want you to be the best you can be." As I tried to obey, God began to open some supernatural doors for *Table Talk* to air on A&E, FYI, and other secular TV stations. Amazing things started happening here at Daystar.

One interesting thing about storms is that they do pass. You are going to come out on the other side, and you're going to be changed. Those experiences definitely leave a mark on your life. But I want you to know something: there are brighter days ahead. God still has more plans for my life, and He has more plans for your life. The Lord says in my favorite Bible verse, Jeremiah 29:11, "I know the thoughts that I think toward you, says the LORD, thoughts of peace and not of evil, to give you a future and a hope."

God restored my heart and gave me excitement for the things ahead. It wasn't an easy journey to get through, but I promise you, God was there. That's what I want you to take away from my story. God is right there. He's with you in the middle of the storm. So cling tightly to Him because He's the One who is going to guide you through. And remember, if you're in the middle of a storm and everything seems hopeless, you're not alone.

STEPS THROUGH THE STORM

Let us run with endurance the race that is set before us, looking unto Jesus, the author and finisher of our faith.

—HEBREWS 12:1–2

The most important thing in life is not how you start but how you finish. Having your eyes firmly set on the end goal instills in you the courage to endure the storms you encounter as you run this race. When you are locked in on the finish line, you are actually locked in on Jesus.

Jesus is standing at the finish line, and He is the finish line. Our ultimate goal is to collapse in His arms and hear Him say, "Well done, good and faithful servant" (Matt. 25:23). Finishing well confirms the authenticity of your faith and leaves a legacy for those who remain. But it starts long before old age. Those who finish well have a focused mindset and have let the Lord guide their whole lives. That's a rich legacy. And only through an intimate relationship with God can we ever really hope to finish well so that, like the apostle Paul, we can say, "I have fought a good fight, I have finished my course, and I have kept the faith" (2 Tim. 4:7, MEV).

> *Lord, You said I could be "confident of this very thing, that He who has begun a good work in (me) will complete it until the day of Jesus Christ" (Phil. 1:6). I cling to that promise. Help me run my race with my eyes fixed firmly on You. Amen.*

Chapter 11

THE SHIFT

THE ENTIRE SEVENTH month after Marcus died, which was June of 2022, the Lord was doing something in me. A shift was taking place; I just didn't know all that it involved. The Lord had been not only healing my grief but also preparing and refocusing me. When Romans 8:28 says, "All things work together for good to those who love God, to those who are the called according to His purpose," does that include the death of a spouse? As I said earlier, if *all things* really means *all things*, then it includes even something as painful as the death of a loved one.

God is using and working everything—even the painful things and things we don't understand—for our good. God, who is outside time and sees the beginning from the end, was working my situation for my good and His purpose. One prominent theologian said, "One of the most amazing and miraculous things about God is His ability to take all the billion possible scenarios, events that happen, and free will, and somehow work them together to fulfill His purposes in us."

I mentioned earlier that I've interviewed people who had supernatural encounters, including near-death experiences. I want to tell you about a man named Bob Bell. His incredible near-death experience directly relates to my story and the storms we go through. Before I share it, I need to give you some information about his background so you'll understand how credible he is.

Bob has been a JAG officer (attorney) handling cases for the US Navy for more than thirty years. He also worked as a civilian trial lawyer, representing numerous high-profile insurance companies, including Lloyd's of London. Professional and highly educated, Bob graduated from Emory University School of Law, one of the top law schools in the country. He was also on the board of governors for his state and even ran for Senate.

Bob is about as solid as they come. He has absolutely no motive to concoct, embellish, or even reveal the details of his story. In fact, Bob would rather *not* tell his story at all because he's aware that many people will look at him with raised eyebrows. Yet he feels compelled to share his story because it brings hope and comfort to hurting people. It also shows that God is real, knows each of us intimately, and is working in our lives even though we often don't understand our current circumstances. Bob is also personal friends with a writer friend of mine who interviewed him on several occasions. With tears in his eyes, Bob described what he calls the most real experience of his life, something just as real and solid as this world, "only in another dimension," he said.

Bob, his wife, and their two-and-a-half-year-old daughter were hit head-on one night by a speeding drunk driver in a pickup truck. They were in a small car. At the moment of impact, a brilliant beam of light shot down from the sky like a massive searchlight. All three died at the scene. "Immediately...I somehow saw my precious wife as her spirit separated from her physical body," Bob said. "Her new body glowed with radiant energy. Then, I saw [my daughter]. She, too, had separated from her physical body and was playing around her mother. I realized at that moment that I, too, had separated from my physical body and was free of pain."[1]

As the three of them traveled in the light, Bob watched both his wife and his daughter disappear into the light. Emanating from the light they disappeared into were sounds of music, celebration, and joy. At that moment, a massive angel appeared between Bob and his loved ones and said, "Stop...your time has not come yet. You still have work to be done on earth."[2]

Bob was shocked. "Why can't I die and be with my wife and daughter?" he asked, pleading pathetically with the angel to let him go into heaven. He didn't want to continue life without his family. Then the angel showed Bob some things about his new future. He told him if he didn't return, many clients would lose their cases because there was no other lawyer to help them. He was told he would have an important role in national defense at the Pentagon as a Navy commander who would save the world from nuclear disaster. He was also told he would be instrumental in catching and convicting the drunk driver who hit his family, a person who otherwise would get away.

Then something even more remarkable happened. The angel told Bob, "You will not be alone and can have another family if you want." This made Bob even angrier. "I did not want to hear that because I wanted the family I already had!" he said. But the angel calmly told him, "If you want to see her, look over there to your left."[3]

Bob turned and saw a vision of a young blonde woman, kneeling, looking up toward heaven, and praying fervently.

What appeared to be bright moonlight highlighted her profile from a side view. In an instant she vanished. When Bob returned to his body, he was covered up in the coroner's van on the way to the morgue. When he began to speak, the driver freaked out!

Some years later Bob was at an event, and there she was—the woman in the vision. Light was radiating off her profile exactly as he'd seen. Though they had just met, they felt uniquely drawn together. They had a navy wedding under an arch of swords, with an admiral holding one of the swords. They've been married for many years and now have three grown children. Just as the angel said, God gave Bob a new family. This in no way diminished his love for his first wife and child. It just shows how God, outside of time, knows everything about us and cares for each one of us. (You can read Bob's complete story in detail in his book *Between Life and Eternity*.)

I can so relate to this story. Bob Bell wasn't interested in a new wife, but he knew God had a mission for his life, and that mission involved a new beginning with a new person. Like Bob, I was surely devastated by my spouse's death, but my mission wasn't over even though Marcus was gone. The Lord had been giving me a vision of where He wanted to take Daystar. Even before Marcus left us, the Lord had been moving me to step out of just hosting Christian TV and reach into the world to minister to lost souls.

Daystar is a Christian TV network that will never compromise the gospel message. Marcus and I built Daystar to reach the world, and at that point, it was available in every country. God's vision for me was to take some of Daystar and deposit it in secular networks such as ABC, Fox, NBC, and CBS to bring the lost over to Daystar and into the kingdom of God. That's another thing that happened through the storm: God clarified this vision for my destiny. It's like blinders fell off and I was totally focused and directed. I sensed a fruitful future for Daystar, but I assumed I'd lead it as a single woman. The thought of remarrying was not even on my radar.

I need to say something important here. Throughout this book I've freely said, "The Lord spoke to me," or, "The Holy Spirit said." Understand that the Word of God is my plumb line. I strongly believe the Lord still speaks directly to people today, yet the Scriptures are our final authority in discerning whether any supernatural experience is from God or from the deceiver. And there is a very real deceiver. While I am convinced God still speaks in a variety of ways, the infallible, inspired Word of God is the plumb line for all truth.

Best-selling author and theologian R. T. Kendall, a dear friend whom I've interviewed on *Table Talk* several times, wrote in his book *Holy Fire*: "Try as I might, I cannot for the life of me twist the text to prove that the power of God in the supernatural gifts of the Holy Spirit was limited to the times of the early church. However, it is not just for me a matter of exegesis, but of personal experience."[4]

In the Book of Acts, the Holy Spirit told Philip, "Go to that chariot and stay near it" (8:29, NIV). And we read later in the same book: "Now when they had gone through Phrygia and the region of Galatia, they were forbidden by the Holy Spirit to preach the word in Asia" (Acts 16:6). Clearly, the Holy Spirit was speaking and directing them. He's still leading and guiding us today. Jesus promised that the Holy Spirit would come inside all believers and abide there forever (John 14:16).

If the Holy Spirit is inside us, He's not going to remain silent. He is the same forever, and He is with us at this moment. He always points to Jesus, illuminates the Word of God, and gives us personal direction. No, the Lord hasn't stopped speaking in a personal way, and He's been speaking to me my whole life with supernatural confirmations. I will share more about that in the final chapters of this book.

From a relationship standpoint I knew I was free, biblically and emotionally, to move forward, but I wasn't looking. There was no real desire in me for a relationship. I want to make that crystal clear. I wasn't looking and had no need to do so. So many people have judged my timeline from Marcus' death to my marriage to Doug. They question how I could have grieved enough in seven months to even think about talking to someone else. They think that's not enough time. All I can say is that each person processes grief differently. For me, this was the timeline I was on. For someone else, it could be very different. Each of us is uniquely created to fulfill the purpose God made us for. We are "fearfully and wonderfully made," as the psalmist wrote (Ps. 139:14). In addition, He has qualified each one of us, meaning He has made us able or authorized us for the task He has put before us.

God was clearly moving on me to head in a specific direction of His calling. This was going to take new tools and actions, but He was equipping me. Anyone close to me during that time knows how deeply I grieved Marcus' death. Words on paper can't express the depth to which I missed him and cherished our times together. Marcus always encouraged me to move out in the ministry God had for me.

Marcus had a kind and loving heart. I can't tell you how many times he told me, in my kids' presence, "Now, sweetheart, if anything ever happened to me, I would want you to get remarried." I would get mad at him and say, "Are you crazy? You're not going anywhere." He knew how much I loved him, but he also didn't want me to be alone. I would tell him I probably wouldn't get remarried. But little did I know how well my husband knew me. His words reverberated in my mind and were comforting to me.

So again, I was free to remarry, but I wasn't looking to do so. That is important to understand. The only way I would be open to marrying again is if the Lord brought someone into my life and then confirmed in an undeniable way that he was the one.

I know you may be wondering what my marriage to Doug has to do with a storm. Why am I even talking about it in this book? I included this part of my story because it brings us back to the reality that obeying God and following His lead often puts us right in the middle of conflict and storms. Going through trials doesn't mean we're out of His will or that we should stop and turn back. It means if we take His hand, He will walk us through to the other side.

For me, moving on meant running right into a storm of judgmentalism—and I'm not talking about judgment from God. You just don't know how nasty "religious" people can be. Some people misread between the lines of articles they find on the internet and fill the space with their own made-up stories. In a self-righteous way, they misapply Scripture to fit their own narratives when they don't have the facts. I'm not talking about godly, biblical correction or counsel; we are supposed to submit to that, and as you will see, Doug and I did. I'm talking about gossip made to sound spiritual.

Of course, when Doug and I began telling people about our relationship, the vast majority said, "We've been praying for you. We're so happy." But the other voices definitely left an impression. For those who may be critical of our relationship or have doubts, I'm asking that you reserve judgment until the end. Then make up your own mind. This is not an attempt to get approval or defend myself; I'm simply telling our story the way it actually went down, including how respected ministers counseled us through a biblical lens.

For those who want to know, I'm telling you so you will be informed of what I went through. I grieved, but I grieved as one with hope, and hope meant I had a future in the Lord. I didn't know what God was going to do, or how or when He was going to do it, or even if He had plans to bring another man into my life. I just told the Lord, "I'm not going to choose that person. If You have someone for me, You'll have to choose him." That's exactly what He did.

STEPS THROUGH THE STORM

Behold, I will do a new thing, now it shall spring forth; shall you not know it? I will even make a road in the wilderness and rivers in the desert.

—ISAIAH 43:19

Whether it's the loss of someone dear to us, a broken relationship, or even an unfulfilled dream, there comes a point when the Lord leads us to embrace with a faith-filled heart the new things that He is birthing in us. Of course we will always remember and cherish the ones we've lost, but we can't remain paralyzed by our pain. That is probably not what your loved one would have wanted, and that's not what God wants.

When we've been through a broken relationship or experienced failure of some kind, fear of dreaming or getting hurt again can stop us in our tracks. But when we are paralyzed and stop moving, we tend to sink into the troubled waters of despair. Accept the Lord's permission to let go, and let Him speak a fresh word into your future. You will gain a new vision for life. It's true. He is about to do something new. Receive it!

> *Lord, I do believe You work all things together for the good of those who love You and are called according to Your purpose—even the tragic things. I thank You that I can trust You to guide me into Your best for me. Speak a fresh word into my spirit and give me courage to embrace the new. Amen.*

Chapter 12

NEW BEGINNINGS

DOUG WEISS, PHD, a renowned, Spirit-filled psychologist, is the founder of Heart to Heart Counseling Center in Colorado Springs and has authored more than forty books. Doug appeared regularly as a guest on Daystar, and we always enjoyed his insight and the way he connected with our audience. That is one reason Daystar was excited to start airing his new show called *Healing Time With Dr. Doug Weiss.* He always had good information and relevant books for our audience, and Marcus and I loved interviewing him. Marcus loved having people call in live and ask Dr. Doug questions. Doug was like most of the other guests we had on regularly in that he would fly in, do our show, and then fly back to his home in the mountains of Colorado.

In June of 2022, in that seventh month after Marcus' passing, Doug called me at Daystar, which I thought was a little odd. Even though he was a regular on our programs, he had never called me personally. Over the years, Marcus and I had sent several couples to Doug for counseling, and he was always a blessing. So when I looked down at my phone and saw his number, I thought, "Huh, I wonder why he's calling me." Most guests or program hosts don't call me directly but instead go through our guest coordinators. If Doug had a new book coming out or something, he wouldn't have called me, so I knew something must be up.

"Hello," I said.

"Hey, Joni. This is Doug Weiss," he said soberly. "I'm actually calling to let you know that I'm divorced."

I was shocked. How could this have happened to this man whom God had used to heal so many marriages?

Doug continued: "I just want to be transparent and ethical about it because you guys are going to start airing *Healing Time*. I don't know how it will affect everything."

All I could think about was how tragic divorce is, and I wondered if his marriage could possibly be healed. I then recommended that Doug go to counseling with someone I knew who had helped several other couples. Without the slightest hesitation or egotism, even though he himself is one of the world's leading Christian psychologists, he said, "Yes, I'll do this." Knowing his program was scheduled to air, Doug wanted to submit to Daystar's protocol.

As Doug was preparing to begin counseling, we exchanged some texts regarding certain details such as what airport to fly into, the addresses and names of counselors, and things like that. I got him connected with the counselor and all set up to go, and that was the extent of our communication.

Doug went through the three-day counseling session and was back home in Colorado by July 4. I texted him and asked how it went. My thoughts were still directed toward the healing of his marriage and how we could continue to help. Anytime a marriage can be saved, that's what I'm hoping for. However, I didn't know the details of his situation other than it had been a long, drawn-out, painful experience.

A couple of the ridiculous lies I heard about Doug and me were that we were somehow connected while Marcus was alive and that Doug divorced his wife so he could marry me. As you will see, that is completely absurd and a lie from the pit of hell. People have thrown out all kinds of creative lies that can also be easily disproved. Some of them will be refuted here as I give you the facts of the situation.

Yes, when I talked to Doug that day, I was thinking about the possibility of his marriage being restored. But then he said, "Joni, I'm divorced, and there are many things you don't know."

I thought, "Wow."

"There's much more to the story I will tell you later when it's appropriate," he said. Later in July, I did learn more of what had been happening for many years, and I realized there was never going to be a reconciliation.

Another one of the lies I've heard is that after Marcus died, Doug went after me. That's completely untrue. At that point, neither of us was thinking about a relationship. We talked about business and ministry.

As the month of July passed one day at a time and I continued to heal, Doug and I started talking and checking in on each other. He was in Colorado, and I was in Dallas. None of this communication took place in person. We'd just check on each other and ask, "How are you doing?" I was still going through changes in the business and my family and so many other areas of life. Doug would encourage me. "You've been through a trauma," he said. It was comforting to talk to him, and we gradually started opening up to each other.

Then, at some point in July, Doug sent a text: "You available to talk?" I found myself getting excited inside and realized, "Yes, I really enjoy talking to him." We talked about the vision God had put in my heart, our kids, life, the Lord, his future, what the Lord was speaking to him about, and all kinds of other things.

Then the Lord told Doug to pray for me every day, so he would call and pray for me over the phone. On other days he would send me an inspiring voice message or prayer in the morning, saying things such as, "Lord Jesus, bless Joni. Help her with wisdom with her show, and give her wisdom with the business and her family and all that she's doing." He would also give me scriptures. People tell you all the time that they are praying for you, but I knew Doug really was, every day, because I could hear his voice or read his text.

Just to clarify, Doug was not looking for someone to date. There had been a lot of water under the bridge—a lot. The divorce was final, and they had been living apart for a while before that. The marriage really was over. We'll get more into the details of that later.

It wasn't a weird thing for the Lord to tell Doug to pray for somebody. He was calling and praying for me as a counselor, a supportive person there to say, "Hey, I hope you're doing OK." We had no preconceived intentions, no desires to have an intimate relationship, and no agendas. We were just friends.

I kept getting those prayers, and as we kept talking, both Doug and I could sense the Lord was doing something, though we weren't sure just what. We're not individuals who would have connected any other way. Doug was still in Colorado at the time, and I was in Dallas. He never had a desire to move back to Dallas, but it just started to feel as though something was up. Doug told me that one time when he was praying for me, he felt as if his heart opened up a little bit and thought, "Lord, what is that?" It was a complete surprise.

For those who say Doug wanted to marry me for Daystar, I ask, Why? He was already on Daystar and already exceptionally successful. He had been on *Oprah, Dr. Phil, 20/20, Good Morning America*—you name it, he'd probably been on it. Plus, the Heart to Heart Counseling Center was thriving. He had everything; he could kick back in the mountains and do life at his own pace. In fact, the Lord was shifting his heart away from counseling to pure evangelism. Doug didn't realize it at the time, but the Lord was setting him up for the next chapter of his life.

The original reason Doug called was that his program was scheduled to air on Daystar and he didn't know if being divorced would cause me as the head of Daystar to say, "Well, you know what? We don't need to do your program right now. You're a marriage guy. This is not going to work." Of course I didn't say that, because I've known him for so many years. I knew his character and integrity, so a divorce wouldn't have precluded him from being on Daystar.

Doug had no desire or ulterior motives about being on Daystar outside of his own program and a desire to help those who were hurting. He never took advantage of our relationship. There was no agenda. That's why when we got married and some people believed that lie, Doug voluntarily took a polygraph test to affirm his integrity. There was absolutely no truth to that claim. We will talk more about the polygraph test later. Our meeting and relationship progression was so innocent. That is what's so crazy about it. And we would also get supernatural confirmation. Keep reading.

The timing was so crucial in the way God brought us together because I wasn't looking, and he wasn't looking. After the divorce was final, Doug was at peace. In Doug's own words:

> I just wanted to please God, and I was now in a different status. Then shortly thereafter, I was asking the Lord, "What am I supposed to do?" He said, "Don't hunt," and I knew exactly what He meant. "Don't hunt for women. Don't go looking. I got this."
>
> "OK, God," I said. "I can do that." And so that's where we were both at. I wasn't looking, and she wasn't looking.[1]

When I started talking to Doug, number one, I knew he was a man of character and integrity. I knew he loved God. I was shocked he went through a divorce and knew there had to be some legitimate reason. But we just enjoyed each other for the whole month of July. We talked via FaceTime and shared worship songs, and his prayers were a blessing to me every morning. Then, toward the end of July, we both felt as though God was doing something, but you have to be with someone to know if there's more happening. We decided we would like to see each other to find out whether what we were feeling was real or not. That's when the opportunity came up for us to go to New York City—chaperoned, of course.

The first week of August, Doug and I traveled to New York City and had an amazing time. I remember the first time I saw him. I thought, "Oh my goodness," and my heart fluttered. I immediately felt I really liked him, but I had never looked at him that way, ever. It was as if a veil had been lifted off my eyes and I was seeing him for the first time. I realized, "I really like him!" He was very sweet and polite and had good boundaries, but it was different now because we'd spent all that time talking on the phone.

In Doug's words:

> I felt the Lord say, "I want you to buy her a heart necklace in New York. I want you to take her to the top of the Empire State Building, and that's where your first kiss will be, and you will know."
>
> I said, "OK, Lord."
>
> That meant once we were in Manhattan, I had to find the right store close to the hotel because I had to go pick it up without Joni knowing. After she checked into her room and I checked into mine, I said, "Hey, you go freshen up in your room. I have something I need to do. I'll meet you back in the lobby in a little bit."
>
> She did, and I went down to the jewelry store and bought her a Tiffany's heart necklace. I also picked up a book with a thousand questions that you ask yourself so we could talk on the way. It was really interesting and fun.[2]

About an hour later Doug called and said, "I'm back. Are you ready?" So I went down the escalator, and he was looking up at me and holding a brown bag in his hand. I could tell there was another bag inside, but I didn't try to look or pry. We went to the Empire State Building and toured everything. Doug carried the bag the whole time, and we finally made it all the way to the top. He looked around and found a perfect spot in the corner. It had a magnificent view of the Manhattan skyline, the Hudson River, and Central Park. He leaned in close and gently gave me that first kiss.

It was a fairy-tale moment that many women dream of. We definitely felt something. Then he gave me a beautiful heart necklace to remember the first kiss. Doug wanted it to be special. He told me the Lord told him to do it. I asked him, "What were you thinking when the Lord told you to buy me that necklace and kiss me on the Empire State Building?"

And he said, "That when I kissed her, I would know what I was asking, which was, 'Am I supposed to pursue her?'"

We knew then that this was more than a friendship.

STEPS THROUGH THE STORM

There is no fear in love. But perfect love drives out fear.

—1 JOHN 4:18, NIV

New beginnings can create storms of their own, especially when they involve taking a risk to love. And remember, not all storms are bad. When our emotions are raging, only the Holy Spirit in us can calm us with His peace and give us clarity about His leading, as He did for me in 1980. I had to lay the guy I was dating at the time on the altar so the Lord could bring His best for me. But there's a difference between discerning the Holy Spirit's warning and living in fear.

While we must be wise, establish good boundaries, and not allow others to abuse us, love always involves risk. It's a step of faith. Whether we've been hurt by a good friend, a boyfriend or girlfriend, a spouse, our children or grandchildren, or people at church, loving again is a risk that is always worth taking. Sometimes it takes courage to receive a gift, but we have to keep in mind that "every good gift and every perfect gift is from above" (Jas. 1:17). God is a good gift giver.

> *Lord, I know You are a good gift giver. You are blessing me in unexpected ways and accomplishing Your good will and purpose in my life. You love me and want to bless me with good gifts. Besides You, the best gifts are the people You bring into our lives. Thank You for Your goodness toward me. Amen.*

Chapter 13

SUPERNATURAL CONFIRMATION

O
UR TIME IN New York was special. Doug and I had fun and learned more about each other by spending time together. What girl doesn't want to be surprised by a beautiful heart necklace and then have a first kiss that sparks something in both of you? Yet as wonderful as it was, I still needed additional confirmation. Though Doug and I would move forward with baby steps in our relationship, I still had to take him to the Lord and lay him on the altar. If we were meant to be, God would have to make it crystal clear to me.

We returned on Sunday. After I dropped Doug off at the airport, I went back home and decided to go out to the pool. Anyone who knows me well knows I love the water and consider it a good place to pray. This was August in Dallas, and it was really hot. The water was nice and warm, so I just lay on my back and gazed up at the stars. While floating in the calm water after such an eventful couple of days, I began talking to the Lord.

"Lord," I said, "You know I'm Your girl. You have ordered my steps my whole life, and You picked Marcus out for me. I'm coming to You now because if I marry again, You have to pick him out, just like You did with Marcus. If this is not Your will, I need You to show me and stop it now. I just don't want to make a mistake. Your will is important to me. It's everything. If this is Your will, or not Your will, I need You to show me."

Earlier in the year the Lord had given me hints that He might be sending someone my way. Hubie Synn had given me the word right after Marcus' funeral that basically the Lord was going to have to put my heart back together. Then he added, "God's going to put your heart back together, and it's going to be Him doing it."[1] On another occasion, Hubie called with a long prophetic word, part of which said, "The Lord wants to make this very clear to you. He won't let you make a decision that is going to steer you in the wrong direction. He wants you to be comforted knowing that He's holding your hand and He's moving you forward."[2] I did take great comfort in that and rested in the knowledge that the Lord was holding my hand and guiding my steps. But the Lord wasn't done talking to me.

Another time, the Lord used Drenda Keesee to speak to me. She is the mother of the young woman whose thirteen-pound tumor disappeared overnight; I shared her story back in chapter 6. I had interviewed Drenda on *Ministry Now* about her new book, and she was about to go on *Table Talk*. The two of us were sitting on the set alone, waiting, when she said, "I'm so glad that you're here alone because I wanted to talk to you privately."

I said, "OK."

She said, "The Lord spoke to me about you three days ago. The Lord told me that He's going to bring a man into your life and for you not to be afraid and to open your heart."[3] It was similar to Hubie's "God's going to put your heart back together" word.

Drenda knew nothing about what Hubie had told me, and she is also somebody I trust. So, the Lord had given me yet another encouraging word from someone who didn't know anything about Doug and me but is a person whose discernment I trust. However, as I lay in the pool that Sunday night, little did I know that the very next day the Lord would answer my prayer with a big, undeniably supernatural confirmation.

A Divine Confirmation

The next morning, which was Monday, I was sitting in my hair-and-makeup chair at Daystar, getting ready for *Ministry Now*, when Shannon Kelly, our head of security, popped his head in.

"Ma'am," he said, "I need to tell you something."

"Sure, Shannon. What is it?" I responded.

"Well, this may sound strange, but I had a dream about you last night and feel like I am supposed to tell you about it," he said.

"You did?" I asked.

"Yes, ma'am, I did," he said. Now, I knew Shannon was a polite, military-type person not given to nonsense, so I knew I needed to hear him out.

"OK," I said. "Tell me."

"Well, it's personal."

I asked Kennon and Dawn, who were working on my hair and makeup, to excuse me. Then I got up out of my chair, and Shannon and I went into the green room for privacy.

"OK, tell me the dream," I said.

"I believe the Lord is bringing a man in your life," Shannon said. He continued:

> In the dream, it was me, you, and another gentleman, and I was walking in front of you, escorting you down a hallway. You were behind me, and I could tell you were holding hands with this person, and you were very happy. I didn't see his face, but I heard his laugh. His face was blurred out, so I couldn't tell. However, I could tell by your posture, by your body language, that you were happy. You were saying something, and you started laughing.
>
> Well, then the other gentleman started laughing, and when he started laughing, he had a very distinctive laugh. And in my mind I went, "Wait, I know that laugh. That's Doug Weiss." Every time Doug comes here and he laughs, you instantly know who it is, because it fills a room when he laughs. And that's what I heard in my dream. And that's why I was like, "Wait a minute. That's Doug Weiss."
>
> His face never became clear, but I knew who it was simply because of his laughter. And in my dream, we just kept moving forward. When I woke up, I went, "Wait, that was Doug Weiss that was in my dream. He was the guy holding Joni's hand."[4]

I nearly fainted on the inside, but I tried not to show it on the outside. I didn't let Shannon know about the incredible accuracy of his dream at that time. We did later. Later, during an interview for the book, Shannon said:

> I was nervous to tell Joni because to bring something like that to her, I don't know much about Doug's personal life

or history or anything like that. I was hesitant to tell her about it, but the Holy Spirit wouldn't let it go. It takes a lot to make me nervous, but I could tell you one thing: I've never been that nervous before. I mean, think about it. Marcus has died, and you have this dream involving a man to tell your boss.

I was so glad the Lord showed me that because it made me feel safe when Doug started coming around, like God had already shown me. Joni said, "I'm so glad that God gave you the dream; because of you being security and you being protective of me, it gave you peace." I honestly believe that God just gave it to me so I would know change is coming and it's OK. His hand is on this. And that's pretty much what I felt in my spirit that God was telling me by showing me what was going on. Once I talked to Joni and told her about it, He kept impressing on me, "It's OK. Change is coming. My hand is on this."

To be completely open here, Marcus had been a major part of my personal life for over eighteen years. And he was my responsibility; Marcus and Joni were. That man means so much to me. One of the last conversations I had with Mr. Lamb was getting his approval and Joni's approval on the plan about asking my wife to marry me, because she also works here. That is a massive treasure and blessing that God allowed me to have that conversation with him.

That aside, with Joni going through everything during that mourning period, we've been praying for her for a very long time that God would bring joy back in, and God would just help her and keep her moving with supernatural strength, with wisdom and understanding and peace.

And so, to see her go from mourning to joy is a blessing that I really can't express.[5]

A few weeks after that supernatural confirmation, in early September, I was outside in the front of the house, lying on the driveway again, just thanking the Lord. My relationship with Doug was growing, and our destiny was becoming clearer. I said, "Lord, You sent this amazing man. I can't believe You did that."

Then the Lord spoke very clearly in my spirit, "Joni, I never forget obedience." He took me back to 2007 when He'd told me, "Marcus is worth fighting for." And He said, "I remember that you did that. I never forget obedience." That's what the Lord said, "I never forget obedience." Of course, it made me cry. That wasn't an easy storm to navigate, but I obeyed the Lord, and God worked a miracle. It wasn't easy, but I did it, and He remembered.

As we go through life's storms, the Lord will sometimes test us to see if we are submitted and obedient to Him, if we trust Him. We all make choices and are free to choose, but "to obey is better than sacrifice," Samuel proclaimed (1 Sam. 15:22). The Lord loves us and will not force us to do anything. As we position ourselves before Him, listen to the promptings of the Holy Spirit, and draw near to Him, He will lead us in the way we should go. We don't have to be afraid of obeying, because the Lord always has our best interest in mind. As we've already seen, He knows the beginning from the end.

Submitting to God's leading and obeying Him is like walking on the path He has laid out for you. It puts you in the right place at the right time, even though there may be bumps and potholes along the way.

When you understand that God sees time past, present, and future simultaneously and already knows what will come in the future, you realize you can trust Him because you know He has the best plan for you. Recently, since I've been married, there have been moments when I'll get tickled talking to God. I'll say, "Lord, You saw this already. You saw this back when I was lying on the driveway, crying, or floating in the pool, gazing at the stars. You knew my future and what was coming. You knew what was ahead, but all You said to me was, 'Trust Me.'"

After the Lord gave us that powerful confirmation through Shannon's dream, and many other confirmations through men and women of God whom I trust, Doug and I continued to grow our relationship in a variety of ways. I'll discuss some of those ways in the next chapter. Yet as wonderful as the dream confirmation was, and despite how we felt about each other, we would need biblical grounds to move forward. I needed our relationship to line up with the plumb line of truth, and so did some other people in my life.

STEPS THROUGH THE STORM

> Your ears shall hear a word behind you, saying, "This is the way, walk in it," whenever you turn to the right hand or whenever you turn to the left.
>
> —ISAIAH 30:21

Did you know that you are on the verge of a supernatural breakthrough? God is putting your heart back together. Sunrays are breaking through the dark clouds. Maybe there's even a rainbow. You can sense it, but you're still hesitant. You need confirmation—a word from the Lord. Just be honest and ask Him if what you feel is from Him. He will let you know. God has promised, "I will instruct you and teach you in the way you should go; I will counsel you with my loving eye on you" (Ps. 32:8, NIV). The Lord's loving eye is on you. You are the apple of His eye. He wants to lead you, but you must ask for His direction and put yourself in a position to hear Him say, "This is the way, walk in it" (Isa. 30:21).

> Lord, You know all things from the beginning to the end. I ask that You show me the way to go. Lead me by Your Word and with Your voice. I need Your counsel, Lord. Make Your way plain to me. I'm listening. Amen.

Chapter 14

ACCOUNTABILITY

I F YOU'RE STILL wondering why in the world you're reading about my relationship and marriage to Doug in a book about navigating life's storms, let me begin by saying that storms are not always a bad thing. In fact, sometimes storms are needed and good. When there's been a long drought and people are praying for rain, when the rain finally comes, it brings refreshing coolness, much-needed H_2O, and new life. We stand outside amid the perked-up foliage and breathe in the freshness. Kids splash in the puddles. Without the rain the storm blew in, everything would be dry, and the plants would wither and die. The rain is good, even heavy rain, though a flood can be devastating. Still, the same storm that brings the refreshing rain is often accompanied by turbulence that leaves fallen debris, drainage problems, and other similar issues that will need to be addressed.

When Doug came into my life, it felt like a refreshing rain saturating the drought in my soul and bringing a sense of newness. Yet his arrival definitely shook things up. Along with the excitement there was some turbulence and downed limbs, so to speak, that had to be taken care of. But it was so worth it because of the refreshing new life. And I always knew no one would be happier for me than my late husband, whom I adored. It's like Doug was the something I didn't even know I needed or was missing.

Doug's unique calling and character complemented my ministry in a marvelous way. He had spent the last thirty-five years helping heal broken hearts. The Lord is mysterious—wonderfully mysterious. He can use storms to bring in unexpected things, and those things can lead us in surprising new directions. But as I said, this storm left a couple of issues for us to address.

Shortly after some people learned that Doug and I were seeing each other, Shawn Bolz told me the Lord showed him there would be many significant marriages in 2023 and that God was bringing couples together in unusual pairings. Doug and I sure fit that description; we are certainly an unusual pairing.

Marriage was part of our discussion early on because neither of us would invest in a relationship if it wasn't God's will. We both maintained our sexual purity throughout our dating life. I didn't want or need a boyfriend, and Doug didn't want or need a girlfriend. I didn't necessarily enjoy being alone, but I was fine remaining single if that was the Lord's plan for me. Yes, we enjoyed being together, which lifted the loneliness, but we were dating to see if we were meant for marriage, if the Lord was pairing us as a team.

Even with all the prophetic words and the supernatural confirmation through Shannon's dream, I needed more. We needed more. We needed biblical accountability. I couldn't move forward and take the ultimate step without knowing our relationship was scripturally sound. And I wasn't looking for a yes-man to tell me what I wanted to hear. I'm not a teenager; I am a mature woman with grandchildren, a worldwide platform, forty years of ministry, and a vision to reach the lost.

The Lord has been beyond faithful to me. I wasn't going to get involved in a relationship that God forbade—that wasn't going to happen. Plus, I'm surrounded by godly people who are committed to protecting me, not just physically but spiritually as well. I know God hates divorce, mainly because of the pain it causes both parties; it rips families apart. That's one of the reasons Marcus and I worked things out after the affair. During that storm, I listened to the Holy Spirit's guidance, and He said, "He's worth fighting for." And Marcus definitely was worth fighting for.

Some people seeking a divorce don't listen to what the Lord is saying and rebel against His will for that situation. Anytime a marriage can be healed, that should be the first priority. Having said that, divorce happens, and it's not an unpardonable sin. God heals the marriage, or He heals the broken people and gives them new beginnings. That's not an excuse; it's a fact. The Lord is all about bringing wholeness and healing.

In no way am I trying to diminish the seriousness of divorce. God doesn't just ignore it either. If you've been knocked down by the turbulent waters of divorce, the Lord wants to pour His warm, healing oil on your wounds, make you whole, and then set you on your feet again to serve Him in a new and deeper way. As the psalmist said, the Lord "heals the brokenhearted and binds up their wounds" (Ps. 147:3).

Because Doug is divorced, some people have called me an adulteress because I married a divorced man who, in their view, should have stayed with his wife. This was definitely a fallen limb that needed to be picked up. Those who passed that judgment on Doug and me while quoting certain scriptures know nothing about his situation or how long and hard they tried to make it work. Most people who say Christians should never divorce don't understand the deep pain the couple experiences, nor do they understand the Bible's more in-depth teaching concerning grace and divorce. Nonetheless, I needed to know for myself if Doug's divorce was biblical and burn that limb! So I went to my friend Jimmy Evans. I knew he would shoot straight with me, and I wanted his wisdom. I also wanted him to walk alongside Doug and me if he felt our relationship was on firm biblical ground. I told Jimmy everything that had unfolded between Doug and me, and he said, "I'm not going to give my blessing or just take your word for it. I want to talk to him."

Before we go any further, let me tell you a little about Jimmy Evans. For years he's been like a spiritual big brother to me. Actually, he's more than that. Jimmy was a friend of Marcus', and the two played golf together. He officiated at Jonathan and Rebecca's wedding and has been a spiritual adviser to me and Daystar many times. Jimmy is also a beloved pastor in the Dallas area who has been instrumental in mentoring many young men in ministry. Most importantly, though, Jimmy is a biblical scholar of the utmost integrity and character.

Jimmy has been a regular on *Table Talk* and *Ministry Now*;

in fact, I can't tell you how many shows we've done together. He has dealt with countless church situations, helping church boards and pastors who have fallen to pick up the pieces and put the church back together. However, Jimmy became a marriage counselor in 1982 and has been helping couples for more than forty years. Marriage ministry has been his main focus, and he is well known for such books as *The Four Laws of Love*, *Lifelong Love Affair*, and *Marriage on the Rock*.

From the beginning Jimmy told Doug and me, "Marriage is sacred. As a pastor and as a marriage guy, I don't want to encourage anybody to do anything that God won't bless." Jimmy himself knew that he was accountable to God for what he taught and how he counseled. He later confided in me, "Joni, when you came to me and began to talk to me about Doug, I was concerned as your older brother in Christ. My concern was, I don't want anything for you that God won't bless. If I felt like this guy was a bad guy, someone that had divorced without a cause or whatever, I'd chase him off. I don't care what you say; I'd chase him off! I seriously prayed about it because I knew I needed the discernment of the Lord."[1]

I brought Jimmy in at the start of my relationship with Doug, and he immediately called and talked to Doug extensively. Not only did Jimmy and Doug talk, but they also went through several intensive sessions together so Jimmy could determine the biblical credibility of Doug's divorce and whether I could confidently pursue a marriage relationship with God's blessing. Again, what's amazing to me and reflects Doug's character is that just as he submitted to counseling, he willingly submitted to Jimmy's inquiries. That began a number of serious sessions of intense questioning and evaluation. Then, with

Jimmy's guidance, Doug and I worked through a biblical compatibility and relationship development plan, not because we needed permission from anyone to date or marry but to keep us accountable.

Now I want you to hear from Jimmy himself concerning his perspective of divorce after witnessing so much pain and devastation through his many years of counseling. He shared this on an episode of *Table Talk*, and I believe his insights are critical to understanding Doug's situation.

> The tragic thing about marriage is when you see two people together and one person is damaging the other person. We all suffer in marriage. If your husband snores, you suffer. If your wife burns the supper, [you suffer]. We all suffer. But there's a difference between suffering and [neglect]. There's a difference between suffering and damage. One of the ways that you measure damage is, "In your presence [am I] deteriorating as a human?" It's easy to measure [damage] when someone's beating somebody or when someone's just abusing somebody and they've got black eyes and welts and everything. Man or woman, whoever's doing it, that's easy to measure. But it's harder to measure when it's emotional and mental.
>
> In marriage counseling, I had people coming in to me and saying, "My spouse is doing this; my spouse is doing [that]."...And again, it's not a matter of just going through some discomfort or suffering. It's a matter of damage, and some of it was twenty, thirty, forty years' [worth]. As a pastor, as a marriage counselor, I'm sitting there, and they're coming to me, and they're asking me, "Do I stay in this situation?" I'm having to go back to the Word of God because I want to make sure that what I'm [telling

them] is according to the Word of God, and I want to make sure that whatever I'm doing is right before God and something that God will bless. So...I'm not speaking out of a few years of experience, where I've helped a few people. I've helped hundreds of people in very serious circumstances. Some stay and some go.

So when you look in Scripture, Matthew 19, Jesus was asked by the Pharisees, "Can a man divorce his wife for any cause at all?" Now, they meant that....Women were property; they were not equal to men. A man could literally divorce his wife for burning the biscuits. He could divorce her for any reason and just walk her to the door, hand her a piece of paper that said, "I divorce thee." And she [had to leave] without property or children, disgraced. So they were asking for Jesus' blessing. And Jesus said from the beginning it wasn't that way. But He said, "Whoever divorces his wife except for adultery commits adultery and causes her to be an adulterer." [See Matthew 5:32.] Well, the word *adultery* there...means egregious, unrepentant sexual sin.

We all know adultery could be a cause of divorce. But then [in] 1 Corinthians 7, the apostle Paul there is again talking about divorce, and he's talking about a different type of reason for divorce. He's talking about abandonment, when someone abandons you. Now when the apostle Paul went to Corinth, no one was saved. There were 100 percent unbelievers. He starts preaching the gospel, then people began to get saved. Some people were saved; some people weren't saved. Then you had a believer and an unbeliever living in the same home, and they're asking him, "If I'm a believer, should I be with this unbelieving spouse that I have?" And the apostle Paul

[in] 1 Corinthians 7, he's saying, "If you're living with an unbelieving spouse and they're willing to live with you, fine, stay. But if they're not willing to live with you, then you're free to go because God hasn't called us to bondage but to peace."

So I have people over the years coming to me who are being physically, emotionally, and mentally abused, and they're asking me, "Do I stay?" Now again, I'm not talking about discomfort. I'm not talking about suffering. I'm talking about these people are suicidal. These people are hopeless; they're distraught, and the person who's doing this to them intends to do this to them and never intends to stop. It is damaging....

So now as a marriage counselor in hundreds and hundreds of real-life situations with people that I've seen just go through hell in a personal way; they're hopeless. Many of them are suicidal, and the person doing it to them is going to keep doing it to them. It's not just physical. That's easy to measure, the physical, but the mental and emotional. And I began to go to the Lord. And here's what they would say to me; hopelessly, they would say, "But they're a Christian," meaning they're bound to stay with them. Because Paul here is talking about believers and unbelievers. "But they're a Christian. They're beating the heck out of me, but they're a Christian. They haven't talked to me in twelve years, but they're a Christian. They haven't touched me in fifteen years, but they're Christian. I'm hopeless because I'm trapped in this marriage and I'm a believer, but they're also a believer. If I was just married to an unbeliever..." So I kept going back to the Lord and just saying, "Lord, I don't know what to do because Your Word says 'unbeliever' here."

The Lord said to me one day, "An unbeliever is not just a person who has rejected Me. It's a person who will not believe. They will not put faith in their situation for Me to act." In other words, a person who's beating you is not a believer. They may say, "I walked down [a church aisle] when I was thirteen years old." If you were truly a believer, you wouldn't be beating a person up, right? If you were truly a believer, you would not be being mentally cruel to this person, and controlling and abusing this person the way you're doing it. When [the Lord] said that to me, that helped, because I was then able to say to these people who had been abandoned—the issue here is abandonment—"If they abandon you, you're free. Now, if they're going to live with you, that's fine." In other words, if you're married to an unbeliever but they're kind and they're nice people and they're not doing you any damage, stay with them, because your children are sanctified because of that. That's what Paul's saying.

But if they won't live with you—there are different ways of telling a person you won't live with them. One way is just to pack your suitcase and leave. You just got abandoned. It's very painful, but it's easy to measure. But another way to say to a person that I won't live with you is to beat them up. Another way to say to a person I won't live with you is you just emotionally detach. You just emotionally, mentally abandon the relationship [by withholding affection, withdrawing sexual intimacy] or begin to be cruel to them or whatever.[2]

When Jimmy first started talking to Doug, he was trying to measure if he was just another guy who was experiencing some marital problems and wanted out. Doug had submitted himself to Jimmy like someone might submit to a priest. Jimmy was questioning him and, in essence, doing what a priest would do in Scripture. If you had a disease, you had to go to the priest, and the priest would determine whether that disease made you clean or unclean. Jimmy was evaluating the disease in Doug's past marriage, and he assessed that the divorce was justifiable.

I can't go into all the messy details, for obvious reasons, but over time Jimmy became convinced beyond a shadow of a doubt that there was biblical justification for Doug to leave. The marriage was not something he'd left easily or quickly. After decades with no change, Doug reached a breaking point. He felt he had only a few options: cheat, divorce, or someone ends up dead. Doug said, "I wasn't going to cheat, and I wasn't going to kill myself or her, so the only other option was divorce. I couldn't go on." When a person gets to that point, Jimmy said, "You know there's pain that's gone on for too long."

Doug said he grieved the loss of his marriage months before he actually divorced "because I knew it was coming," he said. "In my heart, I could just tell. My heart died; it just died. So I was just grieving the loss of business, the loss of ministry, the loss of reputation, the potential loss of family, being misunderstood, being criticized. I dealt with all that stuff before I even filed. God took me through the grief processes in different locations as I was traveling, and He just said, 'Go ahead and deal with this.' That was the summer of 2021. So the grieving was done before I even filed for divorce. I didn't fall to pornography; I didn't fall to anything, so I never struggled with guilt or shame because I didn't do anything like that. I knew in my heart that no one could ever say I didn't take my pain and help thousands of people. When I got divorced, I felt free from the beginning. That's why God probably told me not to hunt [for a wife], because I felt free to hunt. He was like, 'No, don't hunt.' It was the hardest decision ever."[3]

At the end of his sessions with Doug, Jimmy said: "You guys have been accountable to me since we started this journey. I know everything involved in this situation and believe Doug is a man of integrity. I believe he is a godly man, and I believe this is a relationship that God's going to bless."[4] Trust me on this. Jimmy Evans is not going to say something like that if he doesn't mean it. I've known him too long. He would have had zero problem shutting us down if he thought for a moment that Doug was not justified in getting divorced. He has too much integrity and too much on the line.

After that Jimmy walked with Doug and me through the dating process. As I mentioned, with Jimmy's guidance Doug and I worked through a biblical compatibility and relationship development plan. We continued praying and reading Scripture together, as well as sharing two feelings we were having and giving two praises about the other person every day, a practice Doug encourages in his book *Intimacy*. We did this every day, and we still do. We built our connection this way.

Doug and I have probably answered almost a thousand questions in marriage books—again, not because we had to or needed permission from anyone, but for accountability. Putting these disciplines in place helped our relationship grow exponentially. Because we were sharing our feelings, asking each other questions about each other, and reading Scripture, we were really getting close. However, we were both committed to sexual purity from the very beginning, so that was not on the table, and we protected that area of our lives.

Because we were committed to accountability, Doug voluntarily took and passed a polygraph test days before the wedding. Due to what he does for a living, he takes a polygraph test annually anyway. Every year or year and a half, all the clinicians at Heart to Heart Counseling Center take polygraph tests from an independent polygrapher because if they are not sexually pure, they shouldn't be helping people with sexual addiction issues. He included a question asking if he had any romantic interest or interaction with me before that call in June 2022, and the polygraph proved he didn't, which was important for us to show.

Doug and I continued building our relationship through a sound, godly process. Then, on New Year's Eve, Doug proposed to me at the Broadmoor in Colorado Springs. We were married on June 10, 2023. Jimmy Evans officiated at our wedding and said, "In forty years of ministry of doing marriages and helping couples across the country, well, I have never seen a couple walk through a relationship with such integrity."[5]

One of the Scripture passages we used at our wedding and that has become a foundation of our marriage is 1 Corinthians 13:4–7: "Love suffers long and is kind; love does not envy; love does not parade itself, is not puffed up; does not behave rudely, does not seek its own, is not provoked, thinks no evil; does not rejoice in iniquity, but rejoices in the truth; bears all things, believes all things, hopes all things, endures all things."

People want to compare my relationship with Doug with

my relationship with Marcus, but they are two completely different people. I spent more than forty years with Marcus; we had children together and built what is now one of the largest Christian television networks in the world. And yes, we've had some storms, but the Lord always walked us through them, and we had many, many more good times than bad. I loved Marcus, and he loved me. After he died, I didn't know if I could ever love again. But it's pretty amazing how the Lord can put broken hearts and lives together. That's what He did with my heart, just as Hubie Synn prophesied.

Everyone around me has noticed that I am happy. I didn't know I could be this happy again. Doug and I are both surprised by how happy and fulfilled we are and that God put us together. After the storm, not only did God send the refreshing rain of Doug's and my relationship with all its blessings—the encouragement, the nurturing, the time we spent together in the Word and prayer each day—but He also refined our vision. Sometimes you think you're created for a certain purpose, but after the storm the Lord clarifies your destiny and the next steps of your journey.

That's what happened to me. Daystar is staying true to its purpose of reaching the lost, preaching the gospel, and healing the brokenhearted. New doors of opportunity have launched us into the secular arena to reach those who may not know God's unfailing love for them. The Lord is faithful. He continues to show up in storm after storm, and He's also in the cool, fresh aftermath, renewing and refreshing our souls. If you are in a painful life situation or relationship, put your faith in God and trust Him to act.

STEPS THROUGH THE STORM

> The LORD is close to the brokenhearted and saves
> those who are crushed in spirit.
>
> —PSALM 34:18, NIV

There's nothing as painful as the storm of a broken heart. It shuts you down. The pain is so intense that your prayers are reduced to, "God, help me!"—if you can pray at all. You can be brokenhearted for a myriad of reasons. Whatever the issue, "The LORD is close to the brokenhearted and saves those who are crushed in spirit." Did you get that? If you are brokenhearted, the Lord is close to you. He is not far away, even if you feel He is, and He saves those who are crushed in spirit.

The Lord who created you is saving you in this storm. He's not going to let you drown. He is as close as a breath. Just reach out and grab His hand and let Him be your source of emotional security, healing, and hope. It's worth repeating: "He heals the brokenhearted and binds up their wounds" (Ps. 147:3). Like a loving parent, the Lord is carefully tending to the wounds of your heart.

> *Lord, You know I'm hurting, but I feel far from You and hear only a cold silence when I cry out to You. I know You are present, as close as my breath. I'm reaching out to grab the hem of Your garment. Bring Your comfort. Bind and heal my broken heart. Comfort me so I can be a conduit of comfort to others. Amen.*

Chapter 15

JUST TALK TO HIM

WHEN YOU'RE IN the middle of a storm, the one thing the enemy will try to do is keep you from running to Jesus. Fear, panic, and anxiety set in. You have trouble keeping your mind from conjuring up the worst-case scenarios. A storm will do one of two things: it will drive you closer to the Lord, or it will drive you away from Him. The choice is yours.

Some people get angry and bitter, even at God, because of the painful circumstances they find themselves in. When they don't understand, they pull away and shut God out instead of reaching up through the turbulent waves for His hand. The enemy wants to keep you in fear or distracted by your situation because drawing closer to the Lord in those hard times is how we ultimately find comfort and strength. Those who call out to Jesus let the turbulent waves push them closer to God. Often they learn to do this after going through multiple storms in life and experiencing God's faithfulness time and again.

I'm just a down-to-earth Southern girl. I have flaws. I've made my share of mistakes. Yet one thing I have done consistently throughout the storms in my life is talk to the Lord.

I don't always know what the Lord is doing or understand things that hit me out of left field, but I've learned that I can trust Him because He's come through for me so many times. Trusting God is not a theoretical concept for me; it's my life. God is so alive to me in my everyday life, which is why I talk to Him like I'm taking to my best friend. He is my best friend.

I stay in an attitude of prayer, so I'm in an ongoing conversation with God, one that never stops. The Bible says to "pray without ceasing" (1 Thess. 5:17). God doesn't want to be part of your life; He wants to be your life, "for in Him we live and move and have our being" (Acts 17:28).

God lets us ask Him anything. I often say, "Lord, here we are again. I need to hear from You. Where do we go from here?" I know that wherever I go, He is with me, guiding me. Just as the Israelites followed the cloud by day and the fire by night when they were in the desert, I want Him leading me, every step. I'm not leading Him; He's leading me, and I'm following Him because He knows where I'm going and I don't.

One indication that you're walking with God is that you feel His supernatural peace—a peace that passes all understanding (Phil. 4:7). That means it's a peace that doesn't make sense at times. Peace isn't the absence of difficulty or pain; it's the presence of God amid those difficulties. Peace is a person in the storm with us, holding us, carrying us, and calming the turbulence within us. The Bible says, "For He Himself is our peace" (Eph. 2:14). And the psalmist wrote, "God is our refuge and strength, a very present help in trouble. Therefore we will not fear though the earth gives way, though the mountains be moved into the heart of the sea" (Ps. 46:1–2, ESV). Jesus *is* God. He is our peace. Run to Him for refuge, strength, and peace.

He's real, alive, and fully present, even though our circumstances often scream the opposite.

Only the Lord can give us peace and strength in the midst of our storms. If I were to tell you otherwise, I'd be misrepresenting myself and the Lord. From an early age I started walking, talking, and singing with Jesus. I thought that was just a normal thing for Christians to do. I assumed if He loved me and lived inside me, He wanted to talk to me. And I was right! If Jesus wants to live inside me through the Holy Spirit, why wouldn't He want to speak to me? Henry Blackaby wrote in his classic book *Experiencing God*: "God speaks to His people. When He speaks, what does He reveal? Throughout the Scriptures when God spoke, it was to reveal something about Himself, His purposes, or His ways. God's revelations are designed to bring you into a love relationship with Him."[1]

A love relationship with God. It sounds so simple because it is simple! God's ways are not complicated. Jesus said unless we become as little children, we can't enter the kingdom of heaven (Matt. 18:3). The kingdom of heaven is more than an eternal realm. It's a love relationship with Jesus here and now. Praying to the Father, Jesus said, "And this is eternal life, that they may know You, the only true God, and Jesus Christ whom You have sent" (John 17:3). Real, eternal life starts with knowing the Lord and is sustained through knowing Him, and to delve into the depths of that relationship with Him we must become as little children. That doesn't mean we are to be childish or naive. There is a difference. Being like little children means running to Him, hopping in His lap, enjoying His presence, and talking to Him. I guess I've always been a child at heart when it comes to my faith. I often say, "Lord, it's Joni here—Your girl."

As we grow older, however, and life gets tougher and more hectic, we make our relationship with God more complicated than it should be. Just talk to Him and continue to talk to Him. That's what He asks. He sees and hears. He can handle our questions and emotions. He created us to be in a personal relationship with Him. Don't shut Him out. Run to Him and talk to Him, especially during the storms. This is how we develop the kind of intimate fellowship with the Lord that will empower and guide us through every storm we will face.

If you are reading this and don't know Jesus intimately, take a moment and invite Him into your heart. Repeat this prayer:

> *Jesus, forgive me. Come into my heart. Be my Lord and Savior. I surrender my life to You. Fill me with Your Holy Spirit. In Jesus' name, amen.*

HE IS SO MUCH BIGGER THAN YOU THINK

Another amazing thing about God is that He can take the most unexpected things, even tragic things, and use them to miraculously change your life to accomplish the new and fresh purposes He has for you. God isn't surprised by anything that happens to us. He has a purpose for our lives and uses the storms to build His character in us. God is infinite and all-knowing, and He does not fit into our little boxes. He can do far more than we think He can do—"exceedingly abundantly above all that we ask or think" (Eph. 3:20).

I never could have imagined my life or ministry without Marcus. Yet when Marcus had completed his race on the earth, the Lord called him home. Through that heartbreaking storm God did something I could not have dreamed up. It was as if one day I was facing the most difficult journey of my life, and the next I was surprised by what God revealed for the next chapter of my life. His plans are always amazing and always good. We just have to trust those plans. Talk to God and listen. His ways and ideas are far better than the ones we have for ourselves. As God said in Isaiah 55:8–9, "For My thoughts are not your thoughts, nor are your ways My ways....For as the heavens are higher than the earth, so are My ways higher than your ways, and My thoughts than your thoughts."

I've always wanted the Lord's best for my life, from way back when I was a child picking up kids for church on the bus with my dad to when I was twenty years old writing that letter surrendering my life to Him. God is faithful to fulfill that which concerns you. If you commit your ways to Him, He will take you at your word. And when He speaks to you, He wants you to obey—not out of fear but out of love for Him. Even when we mess up, He, the almighty God, can turn it around for our good. It's crazy how He can do that.

God's grace, His ways, and His plans are far greater than we can comprehend. He is always at work and never sleeps. Like I said earlier, I don't understand how He does it, but God is able to be fully present with me and every other person throughout time simultaneously without being diminished one little bit. It blows my finite mind.

My other secret weapon when going through a storm is worship. I'm talking about throwing up my hands and praising God at the top of my lungs. It takes faith to believe God is in control and acknowledge Him in the midst of chaos and pain.

It's next to impossible to praise God with your whole heart while harboring fear, doubt, or unbelief. David thought worship was so important that he had worshippers in the temple around the clock. This kind of worship brings joy. When we worship Him, God shows up in our storms, just as He did for Paul and Silas in Acts 16.

After the residents of Jerusalem had finished rebuilding the wall under Nehemiah's leadership, they were all gathered for a day of worship and dedication to the Lord. It had been a long, hard battle as they built with bricks in one hand and swords in the other because of the enemy's constant attacks. Nehemiah exhorted the people, saying, "Do not sorrow, for the joy of the LORD is your strength" (Neh. 8:10). Other translations say, "Do not be grieved" (ESV, MEV), "Don't be sad" (CEB, CEV), or, "Don't be dejected" (NLT). People who were building a wall while keeping one eye out for the enemy, sword in hand, might not have expected to hear a message about joy. But Nehemiah said, "The *joy* of the LORD is your strength" (emphasis added). Get this now. It's important.

The joy of the Lord equals strength. No joy, no strength—just like no worship, no joy. Nehemiah said this in a situation in which the people were facing grief, sorrow, and relentless attacks from their enemies. Of course, Nehemiah wasn't telling us not to grieve or feel sorrow when we experience tragedy or the death of a loved one. Nehemiah was saying our strength comes when we go to the Lord and experience His joy, even in the midst of our grief and sorrow. If we lose our joy in the Lord, we lose our strength. But what does it mean to have joy? It's not being happy and chipper all the time or walking around saying, "Praise the Lord," in heartbreaking situations.

Joy is different from happiness. Happiness is dependent on our circumstances, but we can be filled with joy even in the most turbulent times.

Joy comes from the presence of God, so our strength likewise comes from the presence of God. "In Your presence is fullness of joy," David wrote in Psalm 16:11. We don't have to be moved when the storms rage around us. Our flesh can rest in hope. If there is "fullness of joy" in the Lord's presence and "the joy of the Lord is [our] strength," that means our strength for life and surviving storms is found in God's presence. David knew this well. He knew how it felt when storms and caves and enemies tried to take him out, yet he always sought God's presence for joy and strength.

In Psalm 42, David wrote: "As the deer pants for the water brooks, so pants my soul for You, O God. My soul thirsts for God, for the living God. When shall I come and appear before God? *My tears* have been my food day and night, while they continually say to me, 'Where is your God?'" (vv. 1–3, emphasis added). David shed tears while those around him were saying, "Where is your God?" That's what the enemy will whisper and your flesh will scream when it looks like you're going under. David knew better than to give up. He knew his joy and strength came from being in the Lord's presence, so that's where he ran.

Running into God's presence and finding strength and joy in the middle of the most difficult and painful trials is not some pie-in-the-sky, self-help, positive-thinking gimmick. It's for real life. I'm reminded of the late Corrie ten Boom, who, along with her entire family, was arrested and imprisoned during the Holocaust for hiding and protecting Jews. The ten Boom family was sent to a concentration camp in Scheveningen, and all but three were released: Corrie, her sister Betsie, and their father, Casper. Corrie's father died only ten days after their arrest, but Corrie and her sister, like so many prisoners, were herded onto cattle cars like animals, stripped, and starved.[2] They witnessed people being exterminated and knew they could be next. Betsie eventually died in prison.

I once read a series of quotes attributed to Corrie ten Boom that is incredible considering all the suffering she endured: "Jesus did not promise to change the circumstances around us. He promised great peace and pure joy to those who would learn to believe that God actually controls all things." "When we are powerless to do a thing, it is a great joy that we can come and step inside the ability of Jesus." "Joy runs deeper than despair."[3] What incredible words written by someone who experienced torment most of us can't even fathom. Could this be true? Corrie ten Boom was sustained in the most unimaginable horror by joy that came from the Lord's presence.

If you're in a storm and are at your lowest point, shift your focus to the Lord. Begin to thank Him for who He is, what He has done, and what He will do! I think about the situation with the tower in Dallas. Marcus and I were moving forward in obedience and faith. God had a tower hidden away just for His purposes, to reach people with the good news of Jesus Christ. Although most people thought we were crazy for attempting to build a station in a market as challenging as Dallas, God supernaturally made a way. He is the waymaker. Our thankfulness throws open the door for the hand of God to move. Never underestimate God's supernatural power to accomplish what He has called you to do.

God has us in the right place at the right time for His good purposes, and He has equipped us to do the work He has set before us to do. Through the storms, God revealed things in me that I had not seen or known. I can look back and see that through the storms and snakebites God had a master plan for my life. He was guiding and preparing me for what was coming. Ask the Lord to show you the gift He has put within you, and let Him develop it. It may surprise you. All you have to do is surrender all and be obedient; He will do the rest.

When the storm clouds begin to clear, you will see that God has something new for you. Storms give us an opportunity to learn and grow. They may give us new direction for our lives or a new perspective on our business or ministry. Maybe a new season is around the corner, and you just acquired the tools you need to navigate it. God loves you and wants His best for you. He is working in and through all things to bring about that good thing.

Pause and Listen

You may know what it's like to go through storms of personal betrayal or to think God has let you down. After those kinds of experiences, you may feel as though you'll never trust again. Your flesh screams out for someone to validate how deeply you were wronged. It's in those times that you need to take a little pause and listen. Give the Holy Spirit an opportunity to speak to you. His voice is so quiet and still that you can't hear Him if you're indulging your anger. I don't mean to say you shouldn't feel angry; I mean you shouldn't act out in anger. Ask the Lord what you should do, and listen to Him. Surrender the situation to Him. Pray in the Spirit, and follow His promptings. This makes all the difference in the storm.

One final lesson that the Lord has taught me over and over again while walking through storms is that He will never ever leave me or forsake me. People, friends, coworkers, and even family will disappoint you while you're in the storm. That's why you must keep your eyes on Jesus. He, not the opinions of those who surround you, is your source. You may see seasons shift, changing your relationships with certain individuals. Just as the leaves fall from the trees during winter seasons, change inevitably happens and people naturally fall out of our lives. Not everyone can continue with you on the journey God has mandated for you. That's OK. Bless them and release them. As I've already said, God works *all* things for our good. That includes the relationships in our lives.

During this past year I was so disappointed because some men and women of God whom I'd known and trusted for years didn't have the decency to call me personally to discuss their questions about my personal life or remarriage. Instead they talked among themselves, often believing rumors and lies. I followed up with those who I knew were talking about us, and with the help of the Holy Spirit, I was able to talk with them and answer their questions.

There were also many prominent ministers who called and encouraged me through this journey. Not surprisingly, most of those leaders were men and women of God who were seasoned in ministry and had experienced their share of storms. My point is, don't get caught up trying to please people; instead, purpose to please God, especially when you're in the middle of a storm. Forgive, love, and pray for those who despitefully use you. By doing so, you will continue to have peace through the entirety of the storm. Then, as you exit the storm and move into the sunshine of life, you will have greater clarity and wisdom in the days ahead. Remember, truth always outlives any lie, and God has the final say. He will fight your battles, and He will defend you. Again, the issue is trust—we have to keep our trust in God.

We've talked a lot about Paul in this book. That's because Paul was no stranger to storms. Read his words and think about the pain and discomfort he felt:

> From the Jews five times I received forty stripes minus one. Three times I was beaten with rods; once I was stoned; three times I was shipwrecked; a night and a day I have been in the deep; in journeys often, in perils of waters, in perils of robbers, in perils of my own countrymen, in perils of the Gentiles, in perils in the city, in perils in the wilderness, in perils in the sea, in perils among false brethren; in weariness and toil, in sleeplessness often, in hunger and thirst, in fastings often, in cold and nakedness—besides the other things, what comes upon me daily: my deep concern for all the churches.
> —2 Corinthians 11:24–28

What's interesting is that while Paul definitely experienced pain and negative emotions, he didn't get bitter and complain or blame God. His faith never wavered. In fact, it seemed his faith actually strengthened in storms. Think about it. Paul wrote two-thirds of the New Testament while chained in prison. He was beaten, yet he wrote, "Blessed be the God and Father of our Lord Jesus Christ, the Father of mercies and God of all *comfort*, who *comforts* us in all our tribulation" (2 Cor. 1:3–4, emphasis added).

But where did Paul find comfort? What did that look like in real time? We'll answer that, but let's keep reading.

> We were burdened beyond measure, above strength, so that we despaired even of life. Yes, we had the sentence of death in ourselves.
> —2 CORINTHIANS 1:8–9

Have you ever felt that way? Paul—the man of God, the apostle—was "burdened beyond measure, above strength" and "despaired." He felt "the sentence of death." Those are some pretty real and raw emotions. Paul had so much on his shoulders, more than he could handle. He was weighed down, drained of physical strength to the point of despair. His mind and circumstances told him he was dead.

You know, it's OK to have those difficult emotions. Just don't live there. Paul gives us the answer:

> ...that we should not trust in ourselves but in God who raises the dead, who delivered us from so great a death, and does deliver us; in whom we trust that He will still deliver us.
> —2 CORINTHIANS 1:9–10

The NIV puts it this way: "But this happened that we might not *rely* on ourselves but on God, who raises the dead" (v. 9, emphasis added). What is Paul talking about here? What experiences taught him to depend on God, who raises the dead? We just named them: pressure, pain, despair—*storms*. Storms actually made Paul stronger because he knew that Jesus was risen and present with him even when the circumstances said otherwise. That's comfort. Remember, this is the guy who wrote, "Rejoice always" (1 Thess. 5:16). Paul knew storms, and he knew joy in the midst of them. This is how he could worship after being beaten and thrown in prison with Silas.

If you're in a storm, take a personal inventory. As I've said, being in a storm can be completely out of your control. You may have done nothing wrong. The storm may just be part of life, and the Lord is using it to form His character in you. Job's trials were not the result of his actions or faults. He was just being tested. Jonah, on the other hand, was disobedient and got swallowed by a big fish as a result. God wants each of us to be accountable. When we make mistakes, if we repent, Jesus is faithful to forgive our sins and cleanse us from unrighteousness (1 John 1:9). All we need to do is be honest before the Lord and invite Him in to take away the things that are not pleasing to Him. Surrendering to Him in this way is beyond worth it because He has so much for us to do for His kingdom. We don't want to be weighed down by things that will keep us from receiving His best.

Paul said, "God has not given us a spirit of fear, but of power and of love and of a sound mind" (2 Tim. 1:7). If you spend even a little time listening to the secular news, you're likely going to hear words that strike fear in your heart. If you're not careful, your imagination can run wild and come up with all kinds of scenarios that will likely never happen. God is the opposite of fear. He is our peace, and His voice calms the storm. You can rest in Him, knowing that He holds you in the palm of His hand, even when the storm is raging.

Losing Marcus was a huge storm in my life. Although I knew he was in the arms of Jesus, his death was just so shocking and painful. Then I felt such loneliness. Those who have lost loved ones understand these feelings. All I can say is that God gave me supernatural grace and strength to continue the ministry despite my grief. My family and friends held my arms up along the way.

I thank the Lord for the prophetic words I received that encouraged and fortified me. The Holy Spirit was truly my Comforter. I pray for each person who is hurting, that the Comforter will touch you in a way that encourages you and brings healing to your soul. You can trust God. He is faithful.

Really, it all boils down to this: in John 15, Jesus calls those who follow Him His friends. What did I do in my storms? I called my friends. We cried. We talked. At times we just sat in each other's presence. That's what friends do. That's grace. That's Jesus. He's always the first friend I call, and He's never too busy to answer.

Life isn't about waiting for the storm to pass. It's about learning to dance in the rain.

STEPS THROUGH THE STORM

You rule over the surging sea; when its waves mount up, you still them.

—PSALM 89:9, NIV

In the chaos of our world today the peace of Jesus is a safe refuge for your mind and heart. When you are deeply rooted in Christ, there is no reason to fear the storms. The psalmist said, "You rule over the surging sea; when its waves mount up, you still them" (Ps. 89:9, NIV). Reach for Him! He's right there, and He's in control. Like the apostle Paul, a man who knew a thing or two about storms, "I pray that God, the source of hope, will fill you completely with joy and peace because you trust in him. Then you will overflow with confident hope through the power of the Holy Spirit" (Rom. 15:13, NLT). Amen!

> *Lord, I need You in the midst of my chaos. I know You are right here by my side, and I trust You. I can't see You, but You see me. Your Holy Spirit is inside me, filling me with hope, joy, peace, and power. That's why I talk to You confidently as I walk through this storm, because I know You hear and will answer. Amen.*

A WORD FROM DOUG

BEFORE THIS BOOK comes to a close, I wanted to say a few words about Joni as it relates to life's storms, things she wouldn't say about herself. Personally, I'm no stranger to the storms of life. I was conceived in adultery, never knew my father, and went into foster care for a while. After living a life of rebellion, drug and alcohol abuse, and promiscuity, I came to the absolute end of myself. At the young age of nineteen, I decided I was going to commit suicide.

Somehow by God's grace I ended up at a church camp, where I found myself kneeling down, praying: "I believe in You, God, but I'll give You thirty days. If You don't show up, I'm going to kill myself." Well, the short answer is, God answered that prayer and showed up in a profound way. He radically changed my life and called me into ministry. Over the years, the Lord has been beyond faithful, seeing me through countless storms and eventually leading me to Joni.

Honestly, Joni has been a breath of fresh air. She came into my life unexpectedly when I wasn't even looking, but each day that I'm with her, I learn afresh how much of a godsend she was and continues to be as my wife and partner in ministry. Her authentic spirit and love for Jesus are contagious. One thing you can be absolutely sure of is Joni is the real deal, and she's all about the gospel. Seeing people come to Jesus is her passion. And oh, she loves worshipping God.

When I think of Joni, an image of a tree comes into my mind. But not just any tree—I see an elegant and mighty Southern live oak with comforting limbs, outstretched and long, almost as if saying, "Come, sit for a while. Rest your weary soul in the shade and take a break from the blistering heat." I'm picturing the Southern states, particularly South Carolina, where Joni was born and raised, with their massive live oaks, many dating back to Civil War times, marking the landscape and lining the streets of their sleepy towns. Over the years the trees have withstood storm after storm and remain standing, a testimony of hope and resilience.

I see Joni as being "like a tree planted by the rivers of water, that brings forth its fruit in its season, whose leaf also shall not wither; and whatever [she] does shall prosper" (Ps. 1:3). Live oaks are considered coastal trees, and based on how they are structured, they are storm resistant. During high-wind situations, even hurricanes, it's rare to see healthy live oak trees down. For example, only four out of seven hundred live oaks on New Orleans' famous St. Charles Avenue were downed by the 175-mile-per-hour winds of Hurricane Katrina.[1]

When they do go down, it's usually because there's some underlying issue inside the tree's wood or roots. As long as they are healthy, they are practically storm resistant. Unlike other trees, the roots of the live oak spread out well beyond their canopy of limbs. This keeps them from toppling over like other trees when the turbulence comes through. Basically, they bend but don't break. That's Joni, forever bending but never breaking, except to be broken before the Lord. She will be the first to tell you that any strength or favor she has is not from her willpower but the Holy Spirit flowing through her branches.

The Lord made Joni perfectly suited to withstand the storms of life. He designed her as a special seed and hid her in a small, remote town in South Carolina, where no one, especially the enemy of God, could pluck the seed out early on as it was beginning to grow and develop. She could grow steadily and healthily in an out-of-the-way environment, putting down deep roots that would eventually grow wide and far-reaching. There, hidden and sheltered from evil influences, surrounded by love and support, Joni was able to fulfill the plans God had for her. He knew she would become a source of encouragement and comfort to people worldwide while advancing His kingdom.

Another amazing thing about live oak trees is they have exceptionally strong wood that is intertwined and dense, making them extremely difficult to split or break. The woven fiber allows the branches and the trunk to be flexible and not snap while the violent wind is yanking them back and forth. During America's early years battleships were constructed out of live oak wood because cannonballs bounced off them. "The U.S.S. Constitution's inner hull (1795) was built from live oak lumber. The strength of the Constitution's live oak structural components was put to the test in battle against the H.M.S. Guerriere during the War of 1812."[2]

The *Constitution* is still afloat today in Boston Harbor. It remains the oldest ship commissioned in the United States Navy. Joni has had to do battle and has taken an array of shots from the enemy, and even some friendly fire, yet she remains resilient. At our wedding her longtime friend Rhonda said: "I met Joni in the summer of 1984. We were two evangelists' wives, and her life was characterized then by two main things: surrender to the Lord and the desire to please Him above all others. In that little room, in that house at Montgomery, [Alabama], we sang with our soundtracks, getting our songs ready to go meet the nations. And we would worship, and we would cry. And her life was always characterized, again, by a desire to please the Lord. And [in] those hours of worship, we found a common ground, and that was it was such an honor to be a part of the kingdom of our Lord Jesus Christ. And from that time on for thirty-nine years, Joni has remained constant."[3] I have found Rhonda's words to be true as I see them play out daily.

As a strong live oak, Joni has the Word of God intertwined in her heart. It makes her steady and has given her courage to withstand the winds that would topple many others. She became a source of strength while swaying but not breaking in the turbulence. Through the different storms, the Joni tree continued to grow, getting even stronger and spreading out a canopy of shade and comfort to all nations. It's really a miracle of grace that only the Lord could do. Joni realizes this. It's bigger than her. Yet I will say that she has allowed the Lord to use her. She consults Him and obeys and is not swayed by people's opinions. Yes, when I see Joni, I think of that lovely, comforting, and strong live oak tree—flexible yet unmovable.

"None of these things move me," Paul wrote in Acts 20:24. What things was he talking about? If you've read this far in the book, you know. To start with, when Paul penned this, he was bound in chains being hauled to Jerusalem, thinking his head could roll. Yet instead of becoming embittered, Paul stayed unmoved and focused on loving Jesus and finishing his course. Why? Because Paul knew Jesus personally and had encountered Him. Paul knew that Jesus was real, alive, and fully present, even in the midst of the storms of life, just as He promised He'd be.

Paul also lived with an eternal perspective, realizing this world was not his final home. "Neither do I count my life dear unto myself," he continued, "only that I might finish my course with joy and the ministry, which I have received of the Lord Jesus, to testify the gospel of the grace of God" (Acts 20:24, JUB). Not only was Paul not moved in the midst of incredible difficulty, but he had joy. This is what God wants to do for us.

When we are focused on knowing the Lord and finishing our course with an eternal perspective, we will experience unexplainable joy in the midst of life's storms. We'll also be empowered with the supernatural ability to not be moved. Isaiah 61:3 says, "They will be called oaks of righteousness, a planting of the LORD for the display of his splendor" (NIV). That's what God has called for all of us, and that's definitely Joni. She's a Southern-grown live oak, flexible in the storms yet unmoved as a testament of the Lord's grace while serving as a canopy of comfort to others. "Friendship is a sheltering tree," wrote Samuel Taylor Coleridge.[4] That's Joni too! All of this is why I love her.

NOTES

CHAPTER 3

1. Dr. David Jeremiah, "Midnight Flurries," Oneplace.com, accessed December 31, 2023, https://www.oneplace. com/ministries/turning-point/read/articles/midnight-flurries-16638.html.
2. T. Neil Davis, "Falling Snowflakes," Geophysical Insitute at the University of Alaska Fairbanks, April 19, 1981, https://www.gi.alaska.edu/alaska-science-forum/falling-snowflakes.
3. Angie Weiland-Crosby, "Winter Quotes & Snow Quotes to Make Your Soul Sparkle," Mom Soul Soothers, accessed December 31, 2023, https://momsoulsoothers. com/winter-quotes-make-soul-sparkle/.
4. Bible Hub, s.v. "grope," accessed December 31, 2023, https://biblehub.com/topical/g/grope.htm.
5. Max Davis, *The Insanity of Unbelief* (Shippensburg, PA: Destiny Image, 2012), 72–74; Bruce Van Natta, *Saved by Angels* (Shippensburg, PA: Destiny Image, 2013), 13–17.
6. A. W. Tozer, *The Pursuit of God* (Camp Hill, PA: WingSpread Publishers, 2006), 57–58.

CHAPTER 4

1. "Peace Be Still," featuring Michael Bethany, MP3 audio, track 3 on Joni Lamb & the Daystar Singers and Band,

No Fear, Venture3Media, 2021, https://music.apple.com/us/album/peace-be-still-feat-joni-lamb-the-daystar-singers/1564046139.

2. Joni Lamb, vocalist, "Peacespeaker," by Geron Davis, recorded 1996, track 10 on He's Been Faithful, Daystar, compact disc. Used with permission.

3. Charles H. Kraft, *Worship: Beyond the Hymnbook* (Eugene, OR: Wipf and Stock, 2015), ix.

Chapter 6

1. Amy Keesee Freudiger, *Healed Overnight* (n.p.: Honest Beauty Publishing, 2016), 99.

2. Freudiger, *Healed Overnight*, 97–99, 113–119.

Chapter 8

1. Charles H. Spurgeon, *The Devotional Classics of C. H. Spurgeon: Morning and Evening I & II* (Lafayette, IN: Sovereign Grace Publishers, 2000), Morning, May 16.

Chapter 9

1. "No Fear," MP3 audio, track 1 on Joni Lamb & the Daystar Singers and Band, *No Fear*, Venture3Media, 2021.

2. "The Coming Threat Series: Pt. 1 | Dr. Michael Yeadon," *Joni Table Talk*, accessed December 31, 2023, https://daystar.tv/player/37118/375044.

3. "Heart Attack and Sudden Cardiac Arrest Differences," American Heart Association, December 2, 2022, https://www.heart.org/en/health-topics/heart-attack/about-heart-attacks/

heart-attack-or-sudden-cardiac-arrest-how-are-they-different.

4. "Mark Twain Quotes About Live Life," AZquotes, accessed December 31, 2023, https://www.azquotes.com/author/14883-Mark_Twain/tag/live-life.

Chapter 10

1. Daystar, "Marcus Lamb Memorial Service: A Legacy of Faith," YouTube, December 7, 2021, https://www.youtube.com/watch?v=h2ujAX8NB2E.

2. Daystar, "Marcus Lamb Memorial Service: A Legacy of Faith."

3. Hubie Synn, in communication with the author, May 2021.

4. Warren Wiersbe, "Warren Wiersbe BE Bible Study Series," BibleGateway, accessed December 31, 2023, https://www.biblegateway.com/resources/wiersbe-be-bible-study/2-my-strength-is-lord-vv-5-8.

Chapter 11

1. Bob Bell, *Between Life and Eternity* (Peoria, AZ: Intermedia Publishing, 2012), 4–5.

2. Bell, *Between Life and Eternity*, 5.

3. Bell, *Between Life and Eternity*, 5, 8–9, 115.

4. R. T. Kendall, *Holy Fire* (Lake Mary, FL: Charisma House, 2014), xxxv.

Chapter 12

1. Doug Weiss, in communication with the author, August 2023.

2. Weiss, in communication with the author, August 2023.

CHAPTER 13

1. Synn, in communication with the author, May 2021.
2. Synn, in communication with the author, May 2021.
3. Drenda Keesee, in communication with the author.
4. Shannon Kelly, in communication with the author, August 2023.
5. Kelly, in communication with the author, August 2023.

CHAPTER 14

1. Jimmy Evans, in communication with the author.
2. "New Seasons | Jimmy Evans," *Joni Table Talk*, accessed December 31, 2023, https://player.daystar.tv/1ITM4kzN.
3. Weiss, in communication with the author.
4. Evans, in communication with the author.
5. Evans, in communication with the author.

CHAPTER 15

1. Henry T. Blackaby and Claude V. King, *Experiencing God* (Nashville: Broadman & Holman, 2004), 153.
2. "Corrie ten Boom," Holocaust Encyclopedia, accessed January 2, 2024, https://encyclopedia.ushmm.org/content/en/article/corrie-ten-boom.
3. AJ, "155 Quotes by Corrie Ten Boom," Elevate Society, accessed December 31, 2023, https://elevatesociety.com/quotes-by-corrie-ten-boom/.

Afterword

1. "Using Live Oak Trees as a Blueprint for Surviving Hurricanes," *Wired*, August 26, 2015, https://www.wired.com/video/watch/think-like-a-tree-using-live-oak-trees-as-a-blueprint-for-surviving-hurricanes.

2. "The Live Oak Tree: A Naval Icon," National Park Service, accessed December 31, 2023, https://www.nps.gov/guis/learn/historyculture/live-oak-naval-icon.htm#:~:text=Constitution's%20inner%20hull%20(1795)%20was,vessel's%20nickname%20%E2%80%9COld%20Ironsides%E2%80%9D.

3. Daystar, "Love's Miracle: A Wedding Special With Dr. Doug Weiss and Joni Lamb," YouTube, October 6, 2023, https://www.youtube.com/watch?v=hD4vxZ0h87c.

4. Samuel Taylor Coleridge, "Youth and Age," Poetry Foundation, accessed December 31, 2023, https://www.poetryfoundation.org/poems/44000/youth-and-age-56d222ebca145.